Golfgames

THE SIDE GAMES WE PLAY & WAGER

RICH USSAK

CONTEMPORARY
BOOKS
CHICAGO

Library of Congress Cataloging-in-Publication Data

Ussak, Rich.
    Golfgames : the side games we play & wager / Rich
Ussak.
        p.   cm.
    Includes index.
    ISBN 0-8092-3799-7
    1. Golf.   2. Golf—Betting.   I. Title.
GV965.U98   1993
796.352—dc20   92-41270
                                                                    CIP

Illustrations by Craig A. Arbon

Published by Contemporary Books, Inc.
Two Prudential Plaza, Chicago, Illinois 60601-6790
Manufactured in the United States of America
International Standard Book Number: 0-8092-3799-7

Dedicated to my parents, Bob and Eileen,
for their continuous support, encouragement,
and love

CONTENTS

ACKNOWLEDGMENTS ix

PREFACE xi

INTRODUCTION xv

THE SIDE GAMES WE PLAY & WAGER:
GROUP ONE 1

THE SIDE GAMES WE PLAY & WAGER:
GROUP TWO 27

TRIVIA 73

THE SIDE GAMES WE PLAY & WAGER:
GROUP THREE 83

THE SIDE GAMES WE PLAY & WAGER:
GROUP FOUR 127

THE 19TH HOLE 155

THE GAMBLING POLICY OF THE UNITED
STATES GOLF ASSOCIATION AND THE
ROYAL AND ANCIENT GOLF CLUB OF
ST. ANDREWS, SCOTLAND 157

INDEX OF GAMES 159

ACKNOWLEDGMENTS

Thanks to Mike Ashurst, who originally planted the seed for the book; Paul MacDonald, for the advice and constructive suggestions; Judi Dickerson and Laurie Cowan, for the help and time spent on WordPerfect; the Boys at De Pals, Costa Brava; Dom "Zeke" Ziccardi, Bill "Cecil" Lindley, and Jim "Bart" Bartlein, who all had games for me to include in the book; and Craig Arbon, partner, whose creativity has enabled us to provide levity as illustrated by "our" players and cartoons.

Thanks also go to Peter Dobereiner, the United Kingdom; Kevin Rejda, Florida; Dennis Verbeek, Texas; Mackie Chapman, Florida; and Ken Smalley, Arizona, who have provided games included in this edition.

A warm and appreciative thanks to all of you, and to the many others who advised me of the side games they play.

PREFACE

It's a game that is played by close to 50 million people around the world. It's a game that knows no boundaries regionally, nationally, or geographically. Whether you are in North America, South America, Europe, Southeast Asia, Australia, or the reputed ancient home of the game, Scotland, the game is immutably the same.

Of course, there are some differences, such as the number of sand traps you have to confront or the number of holes with water that come into play. You may have to play through a veritable forest, or play on a course built in the mountains with so many ups and downs that you think you're a mountain goat. Or possibly you are on a course that has rough so thick and high that you are lucky to find your ball, much less hit it out of the rough. (Was the greens keeper on vacation?)

However, whatever the changes in topography,

vegetation, or scenery you encounter, it's a game that is always played with basically the same rules, equipment, and intentions. Unfortunately, for most of us those intentions are not achieved, and, more often than not, the game just does not turn out the way we had dreamed it would.

That blasted white sphere just didn't go where I wanted it to, didn't break the way I thought it would, or the distance must be wrong! I overshot the green and wound up in heavy rough, or I undershot the green and am now in a sand trap—which, for most amateurs, dredges up nightmares of past sand play. How about the easy chip shot just off the green that you somehow "miss"? You either skull it over the green into the rough or into a sand trap that you weren't even thinking about. Or you stub the chip, "hitting" it so fat that you're lucky if the ball goes a foot or two, much less gets to the green.

What about that 30-foot putt that's facing you with or without break, and since you didn't have your Wheaties that morning, your putt barely gets halfway to the hole? Or, maybe you *did* have your Wheaties that morning, so your putt goes 15 feet by the hole— why didn't that one drop? Or what about when you have the hands and touch of a gorilla on a particular day to the point that you're even nervous about the two- and three-foot putts?

Maybe you're on the tee and have been driving well all day but on this tee shot you "duck" it really bad to the left. Perhaps you don't have a swing in which you hook the ball but, instead, you have a swing that produces the big banana ball, otherwise known as the "slice." Or maybe you've hit your tee shot so badly you almost whiffed. You did make contact with the top eighth of the ball and dribbled it off the tee though, and it did go straight.

It's a game in which you can go out one day and come back another and say either "How the hell can I shoot that bad after scoring so well before?" or "What the hell did I do right? I haven't played that well in a long time."

It's a most frustrating game in which one is bound eventually to hear all sorts of expletives, some of which might even be new. It's a game in which you might be playing with a friend who is usually quite calm, one who never gets angry, but after hitting a real bad shot starts cursing a blue streak; then you hear whomp—whomp—whomp—whomp, which is sometimes called the helicopter but is more commonly known as the thrown club. It's a game that changes people's personalities and demeanors. It's a game that you truly cannot predict. It's a game that keeps us coming back for more of the challenge of doing what we want to or hope to with that small white sphere.

However, this game is unlike any other in that there can be a so-called parity among players, and that parity is achieved through utilization of a handicap system that is based on scoring versus par. This system basically computes your proficiency (or lack thereof) determined by the scores that you have shot and how those rounds compare to par. Par is that elevated plateau that tells one that the ball should be struck or putted no more than x number of times before the ball should be in the four-and-one-quarter-inch-diameter hole in the ground called the cup. If you end up in the cup in fewer than x, you are under par; if you end up in the cup in more than x, you are over par. The latter probably applies to over 99 percent of all those who play the game.

As a result of this unique system, a whole world of permutations of how the game can be played has evolved. The traditional medal play for the most part has been supplanted by match play, Nassaus, best balls, high ball/low ball, and many more variations. They all allow players of different levels of proficiency to compete against each other based upon those differences in level of play and, for the most part, based upon handicap. There are of course other forms of play that do not involve handicaps. However, one reason we all keep coming back to best that white sphere is the friendly competition that invariably accompanies a round of play and that, in one form or another, involves wagering.

It can involve just a friendly purchase of a drink for the winner by the loser, or the loser may buy dinner and drinks! Or it can involve a dime a point, a dollar a point, five dollars a side, or a dollar a yard per hole. The games that can be played and the stakes or bets vary as much as one's imagination will allow.

That's what this brief book is all about: the games people play and how they play and bet them. As mentioned previously, it is a unique game played throughout the world and one which, for most of us, while supposedly being relaxing or a source of exercise, is frustrating as hell! It's a game called golf, a simple word that in no way portends what is in store for those who choose to play it. I press!

INTRODUCTION

It all started for me when I was a youngster and all my experience with the game of golf was the small putt-putt courses with those impossible anthill or windmill holes. However, at the age of 13 my experiences and vocabulary regarding golf were enhanced when I began caddying at a private club.

As a matter of fact, I started caddying when they came out with those huge golf bags that we called kangaroo bags. Those bags at the time were almost as big as I was, and sure enough, when I began caddying, I invariably wound up carrying one of those monstrosities. Unfortunately, for the most part the golfers with these kangaroo bags played a game that was directly proportional to the size of their bag! At this point I was lucky to just make it through one round of golf, and didn't even dream of carrying two golf bags. Besides, caddying for one person when I didn't know what I was doing was difficult enough.

I did, however, survive those first few weeks of caddying and found out what Epsom salts were and how they soothed sore shoulders. I also learned that my shoulders hurt because those kangaroo bags with all those different compartments carried almost everything under the sun, including dozens of golf balls, dozens and dozens of tees, golf gloves (some of which looked and smelled as if they had died and gone to heaven at least twice), Band-Aids, toothpicks, adhesive tape, spare spikes, ball markers, divot repairers, pencils (some with erasers) and pens, new and old scorecards with past claims to fame of previous great rounds of golf or of that unbelievable eagle or double eagle, spare golf shoes, socks, rain gear and umbrellas, a towel, a book or books on USGA golf rules and regulations, Ben-Gay, some type of sun lotion, bug spray, aspirin, and often a fifth of booze used to build moral confidence or to ease the pain of missing that one- or two-foot putt! I'm sure I've inadvertently left out some item or another, but just thinking about all this is making my shoulders sore!

After caddying for about a month I finally became an official caddie and was given a caddie badge indicating that I was now Caddie 96. I had survived those first weeks and started to actually think about the time when I would be able to carry two golf bags, known as a double loop. However, before that was to happen, I was indoctrinated into a new world of language which changed the meaning of all types of words I thought I knew. Hooks, duck hooks, slices, banana balls, chilly-dipping, skulling the ball, the yips, and the thing called a shank, which even sounded ominous, were a few of the words in this new language. Also, there were other things to learn, such as not stepping in someone's line, marking the ball, tending the pin, replacing that divot, repairing a ball mark, raking the trap, and many more.

It was also during my first month of caddying that I heard members talking about a Nassau, which I thought was a reference to that vacation place in the Caribbean. Then I heard them talking about Skins, which I thought at the time was a reference to the football team or possibly the skins in a skins-versus-shirts basketball game. When the members started to say things like, "I press you," or "We accept your press," and "Double press you," or "That's two tie all tie and therefore your skin has been nullified," I realized how little I understood of their talk.

I did learn fast, but only at the expense of hard-earned money I had made carrying a golf bag around the course. The way I learned was on caddie day (which was always on Mondays, when the course was closed to members for course maintenance) when 20 or 30 caddies got together and played golf for the entire day at no cost except for the bets lost to other caddies. This was where I started to play in the Nassau games, the Skins games, and the Best Ball games, and learned their meanings and how you won or lost. I learned the rules of the game and the variety of games that can be played from the older and more experienced caddies, some of whom were outstanding golfers. When the caddies played they always played the ball down, and with very few exceptions we played the ball as it lay.

In those days, there were some really good golfing caddies and, regardless of how well I played, I could never beat them, even if I played over my head. At times I thought I was the Good Ship Lollipop to those caddies, which aggravated me to no end! In retrospect, I believe they just always negotiated a bet that benefited them more than it did me. However, they were good teachers, and honest.

By the time I was 16 I became what was considered a special caddie, which meant that I was a caddie who knew how to play the game and to a certain extent, through my Monday experiences, knew how to bet the game. I could also "club" a player (advise which club to use), read a green, or possibly even give constructive hints about their golf swing or how to play a shot. At times such advice could be dangerous or detrimental to your tip, depending upon whom you were caddying for: besides possibly being the hero, you could also turn out to be the goat and be declared the reason for an errant or bad shot.

As every golfer knows, golfers have more excuses than there is sand in a sand trap! "I shouldn't have lost to you." "You shouldn't have won." "If I had only hit that shot." "If you hadn't sunk that putt." "If I hadn't hit that ball OB on 18."

From those early golf experiences I did learn to play the game reasonably well, and I also learned to play a lot of the games that we still bet on 25 years later.

To this day I don't have a high level of proficiency, as evidenced by my 14 handicap. However, like most of us, and fortunately so, I don't play the game for a living and therefore really enjoy the game and the action and competition it generates. I hope the same proves true for you.

> *"In golf, as in life, one is confronted with many up-and-down challenges, and those who address them learn and eventually gain from those experiences."*
>
> —R.U.

Golfgames

The Players :

Skins Niblick · Shagbag · Mother Irons

Partner · The Kid · Angus McDivot

THE SIDE GAMES WE PLAY & WAGER: GROUP ONE

The games covered in this chapter are fairly simple, and though they can be played by themselves, they are usually played in conjunction with other games covered in later chapters.

The games involve different aspects of golf, from putting on the practice greens to maintaining tee honors to three-putting a green. Some of the games involve penalizing a player for hitting various types of errant shots, while on the other hand some of the games reward a player for hitting a good shot or for achieving a specific aspect of the game. Most of the games apply to any level of proficiency and all players can be involved. Therefore the following should provide you with the opportunity to introduce some friendly but fun competition to the round.

GARBARGE

BINGO-BANGO-BONGO (BINGLE-BANGLE-BUNGLE)

GREENIES, PLONKERS, BLUE-PLATE SPECIALS,
or PROXIES

BMWs

CARPETS

CHICKEN AND SNAKE

OUZLE-FOUZLE

18-HOLE GREENIES

SANDIES or GRITTIES

SUPER SANDIES

EXOTIC SANDIES

ARNIES or SEVIES

HOGANS

BARKIES or WOODIES

GARBARGE SKINS

FERRETS or WATSONS

GOLDEN FERRETS

MOLES

MURPHYS

DOUBLE MURPHYS
NICKLAUSES
SCRUFFIES
TITANIC
ANIMALS
POLEY
FLAGGY
SKINS
SEVEN-UP
LOW PUTTS
SEVEN-ELEVEN
SNAKE
SNAKES
WALK WALK
TEE GAME
RABBIT
RABBITS
TICKS
TWENTY-ONE
UMBRELLA

GARBARGE

This is a term that is used to describe other games that can be played while playing a standard 18-hole match like a Nassau or a Best Ball. In Garbarge, a player or team can win points for achieving a par or a birdie in a variety of fashions, or possibly hitting a shot that is closest to the pin. Since the term *Garbarge* means different things to different players, make sure that you know what the Garbarge is that you are playing for. In some games of Garbarge a player can lose more money than in the 18-hole Nassau or Best Ball game that is being played. The following, from Bingo-Bango-Bongo to Titanic, are some of the types of Garbarge.

BINGO-BANGO-BONGO (BINGLE-BANGLE-BUNGLE)

This is a game in which the individual who is first on the green (Bingo) wins a point, or a quarter, or whatever the stakes. The same is true for the individual who is closest to the pin (Bango) once everyone is on the green, and for the individual who first putts his ball into the cup (Bongo). Thus, first on, closest to the pin, and first in decides who wins on each hole.

> *"Never bet with anyone you meet on the first tee who has a deep suntan, a one-iron in his bag, and squinty eyes."*
> —Dave Marr

GREENIES, PLONKERS, BLUE-PLATE SPECIALS, or PROXIES

These are some of the terms used to describe the player whose shot is closest to the pin on par 3s when hit in regulation. The player who achieves the Greenie wins a point. However, a lot of golfers play that if the player getting the Greenie does not at least par the hole then that Greenie is lost. If a Greenie is lost, or if no player gets a Greenie because no one hit the green in regulation, most golfers play carryovers, so the next par 3 counts for 2 points. Also, some golfers play that if one player gets all the Greenies in a round, the points are doubled in value. When playing partners, such as in a Nassau, it's often common that a player achieving a Greenie gets the Greenie for the team so that each player on the team wins 1 point. Some also play that if the player getting the Greenie putts for a birdie then the point value for that Greenie is doubled. In the case of a carryover where the player getting the Greenie also birdies the hole, then the point value is four times the original. In the event that no player gets a Greenie after playing the par 3s, many golfers play that the second shot to the last par 3, that is closest to the pin, wins all 4 Greenies or points.

"The hole will not come to you, you must go to it!"
—Bob Toski, *Golf Digest*, 1990,
on putts left short

BMWs

Of course this has never happened to you, but I'm sure you've played with others who have thought they have hit a bad shot, mis-hit a shot, or made a bad putt. However, due to the forces of nature, luck, or a member bounce, the supposedly bad shot or mis-hit shot then turned out to be a good shot or somehow that putt dropped in the hole. If this situation occurs—that is, a player bitches, moans, whines, or snivels about his or her shot or putt that then turns out to be good and there is a consensus among the other players, they can call a BMW. The player must then rehit or reputt the shot. So be careful what you say and when you say it!

CARPETS

In the course of playing Greenies, if a player or team wins every Greenie, then the payoff by the other player or team is doubled.

CHICKEN AND SNAKE

This is a game for the practice putting green. With this format, played with two or more, a putt left short of the designated hole costs a point. A putt that misses long and is again missed coming back also loses a point while a one-putt wins a point. Point differentials decide the winner and who pays whom.

OUZLE-FOUZLE

In Scotland and England the player who hits a shot that is closest to the pin on par 3s is said to have won an Ouzle from the other players. However, if the player who won the Ouzle three-putts, then that player is now said to have the Fouzle, and instead of winning a unit or point from the other players, the player now pays the others. So an Ouzle is good and a Fouzle is bad!

18-HOLE GREENIES

In California and some other areas they play Greenies for all 18 holes so that the closest to the pin in the fewest shots by any player in the foursome wins a Greenie.

SANDIES or GRITTIES

This is a term used to describe a player who has hit into a greenside sand trap but still manages to par the hole. For each Sandie a player gets, that player wins 1 point from the other players in the foursome.

SUPER SANDIES

A variation of Sandies in which a player achieves a par or better from a fairway bunker. If playing Sandies, a Super Sandie is worth 2 points.

EXOTIC SANDIES

If playing Sandies and a player achieves par or better after being in both a fairway and a greenside bunker, then that player is said to have achieved an Exotic Sandie and wins 4 points from each of the other players.

ARNIES or SEVIES

These are terms used to describe a player who, with the exception of par 3s, on any hole is never on the fairway but still manages to par the hole. In such an event, that player wins 1 point from each of the other members of the foursome.

HOGANS

In this side game, a player wins 1 point from the other players by achieving a par or better on par 4s and par 5s and never has the ball out of the fairway. This side game does not include par 3s, and greens must be reached in regulation. If you are also playing Arnies or Sevies, which have a point value of 1, then Hogans should have a point value of 2.

BARKIES or WOODIES

These are terms used to describe a player who hits any part of a tree, whether trunk, branch, or limb, and still achieves a par. That player wins 1 point from the other players.

GARBARGE SKINS

In Garbarge Skins, unless a player is tied or someone else shoots a lower score, a player wins 1 point for a par and 2 points for a birdie and collects from each member of the group. (See the more detailed explanation of Skins later in this chapter.)

FERRETS or WATSONS

A player who is off the green and chips into the hole, regardless of score achieved, wins 1 point from the other players.

GOLDEN FERRETS

A player who is in a bunker and holes out, regardless of score achieved, wins 2 points from each of the other players.

MOLES

In this side game, a player who leaves a ball in a bunker after one shot pays the others in the group one bet; if the player leaves the ball in the bunker on the second shot, then the player loses two bets to the others.

MURPHYS

A player who is just off the green and is facing a chip shot can call a Murphy prior to chipping. Once a Murphy is called, the player must then chip and one-putt to win a point from each of the other players. If the Murphy is not achieved, the player loses a point to the others.

DOUBLE MURPHYS

In this case, a player who has called a Murphy but has chipped off the green can now call a Double Murphy, which requires the player to chip and one-putt. If not successful, the player loses another 2 points to each of the other players. If the player does chip and one-putt, the player wins 2 points from the others. However, remember that the player lost 1 point when a Murphy was called, so the player on that hole would win a net 1 point from the others. If the player did not make the Double Murphy, then that player loses 3 points on the hole to each of the others.

NICKLAUSES

These are side bets in which the player in the group that has the longest drive in the fairway wins a point from each of the other players. This is a game played on all par 4s and par 5s.

SCRUFFIES

In this situation a player who hits a really terrible tee shot calls a Scruffy and must then make a par or better on that hole. If a par or better is achieved, then that player wins a point; if not, the player loses a point to the others. If a Scruffy is called, all the other players must agree that the tee shot was indeed terrible.

TITANIC

In this situation a player who hits a shot into the water but still achieves a par or better on the hole wins 1 point from each of the other players.

ANIMALS

In this game, certain types of errant shots are designated as different types of animals. The player with the last Animal during the round of play pays the other players whatever value has been placed on the Animal. Usually each Animal has the same value and in most games that value is $1. A shot hit out of bounds is a Gorilla and a shot hit into the water is a Frog. On courses that don't have water or where water comes into play on only a few holes, any shot that hits a tree is a Tree Frog. A shot that is hit into any sand trap is a Camel, and anyone who has a three-putt has a Snake. In this game the last player to have any Animal or Animals during the round pays the other players.

Additionally, if a player ends up with all four Animals, that player then pays the others double. This game offers additional excitement because no one wants to end up having the Gorilla, the Frog, the Camel, and the Snake!

POLEY

This is a putting game played in the southeastern United States. Any player who sinks a putt that is longer than the length of the flagstick on any hole wins 1 point from each of the other players. If two or more players sink putts longer than the flagstick, they each earn a point. At the end of the round, add up each player's points. The player with the most points wins an amount equal to the point differential between the other players, multiplied by the value of each point.

FLAGGY

This is a side bet in which a player or players win a point for hitting their tee shot on par 3s within flagstick distance of the hole.

> *"If I died . . . it meant I couldn't play golf. No way was I giving up golf, so I gave up drinking."*
> —Bob Hope, *Los Angeles Times*, 1982

SKINS

This game is usually played by a threesome or four-some, and the player who scores a par without being tied or beaten by another player wins a Skin. If a player scores a birdie and no one else scores one, then that player gets 2 Skins for that hole. In this game, if two tie, then all tie. If a player scores an eagle and no one else scores one, then the player gets 3 Skins for that hole. In the case of a player scoring a birdie and each of the other players scoring a par, the birdie shooter is the only one to get a Skin for that hole. This can also be played so that the low score on a hole, providing there are no ties, gets a Skin regardless of whether or not the low score is a par or better.

In this game you can also play carryovers: If no one gets a Skin on a particular hole, then on the next hole the player who gets a Skin also gets a carryover Skin from the previous hole. If four consecutive holes are tied, then the fifth hole will count for 5 Skins if a player wins that hole without being tied.

At some clubs, when we have a large turnout of members, we play a pot Skin game. Everyone who is in the Skins game puts $5 into the pot. After everyone has finished playing, we run down the scores on each hole, and the player who shot a birdie or a par with no other player beating that score or tying it gets 1 Skin. After determining the total number of Skins for the entire group, we divide that number into the worth of the pot to determine the value of each Skin. With 16 players, for instance, where there are only 5 Skins and one player has 2 of the 5 Skins, then each Skin is worth $16 and the player with 2 Skins gets $32 out of the total pot of $80, with the balance going to the other three players with 3 Skins.

With a large number of players with varying handicaps, we sometimes break the Skin game up into two groups, one group playing gross score while the other plays with their handicaps. When a group is not too large, say 12 to 16 players, and there isn't a huge discrepancy in handicaps, everyone will play a net Skin game with full handicaps taken where they fall on the scorecard.

We have also played a Skins game in which we have allowed only an arbitrary maximum handicap of 24 for each individual player; we applied half of everyone's handicap to decide the Skin winners.

In this game the maximum handicap allowed to determine Skins is 12 and the handicap strokes are taken as they fall on the scorecard. Remember that if two tie, then all tie in this game.

"It's Old Man Par and you, match or medal. And Old Man Par is a patient soul, who never shoots a birdie and never incurs a buzzard. He's a patient old soul, Old Man Par. And if you would travel the long route with him, you must be patient too."
—Bobby Jones

SEVEN-UP

This is a putting game that is usually played on the practice putting green while you are waiting to tee off or possibly just practicing your putting with some friends. The game is played with at least two players, and I have played the game with as many as eight.

Points are earned or lost based upon the following: The player closest to the preselected hole after everyone has putted earns 1 point. If a player sinks a putt for a one-putt and no one else does so, the player earns 2 points. Anyone who three-putts on a hole loses 3 points, and the player who has the fewest putts on a hole without being tied earns 1 point. In this game, if two tie, then all tie—with the exception of the players who three-putt. The first player to earn 7 points wins the game and is paid by the other players based upon the difference in their point totals. If two players each earn 7 points, then everyone plays another hole, or more, until one player earns that 8th or 9th point with no other player having the same high-point total. Whoever has honors in this game gets to select the next hole, which could conceivably be on the other side of the putting green, and each player must putt to it. Honors go to the player who earns a point or points on the hole without being tied. The player who has the honors also putts first.

In Seven-Up, since we play with friends, we mark our balls after putting if requested to; however, there are some players who don't allow marking of the ball at any time and play that if you are stymied by another player's ball that's just too bad. As with other games this can be played for 10 cents per point, 50 cents per point, or $1 or more per point.

LOW PUTTS

This is another putting game that is played on the practice putting green. In this game, played by two to eight players, 9 or possibly 18 holes are played, with each player putting to the selected hole and putting out. No gimmies in this game. Select an order of play so that each player gets to select a hole to putt to; the player who selects the hole putts first. The holes selected can require a short putt or a long putt across the practice green to a hole that is 40 to 50 feet away. The winner of this game is the player who has the fewest total putts for the holes that were played. In case of a tie, the players can either split the winnings or can simply have a putt-off.

SEVEN-ELEVEN

This is another putting game but one that involves just two players. This game is also played on the practice putting green, but each player uses two balls, and whoever has the honors putts the first ball and then the second ball to the selected hole, followed by the second player, who putts both balls. Blocking your opponent is perfectly legal in this game, since you do not mark your balls. The closest ball to the hole earns 1 point regardless of whether or not the second ball is farthest from the hole. If, however, both of one player's balls are closer to the hole than the opponent's two balls, then that player earns 2 points. Also, a one-putt earns a player 3 points.

However, if a player has a one-putt and the opponent follows with a one-putt, then the opponent earns

6 points and the first player gets no points on that hole. If the first player has two one-putts and the opponent has none, then the first player earns 6 points. If one player has two one-putts and the opponent has one, then the player with two earns 3 points. In the case of both players sinking both balls for one-putts, then the second player would earn 12 points. In the case of the first player having only one one-putt while the opponent has two one-putts, the opponent would earn 6 points for topping the first player's one-putt but would also earn another 3 points for the second one-putt, for a total of 9 points earned on that one hole.

The first player to earn 11 points wins the game and is paid by the other player based upon the point differential between them. However, if a player earns 7 points before the other player earns even 1, then the game is a shutout and the bet is automatically doubled. Honors, or who putts first, goes to the player who earned points on the previous hole, and whoever has honors in this game does have an advantage over the other player. Remember that in this game blocking your opponent by lagging a putt to block the line of your opponent or blocking the hole to prevent your opponent from one-putting is legal. You don't mark your putts in this game.

"I play with friends, but we don't play friendly games."
                                                        —Ben Hogan, *Golf Digest*, 1970

SNAKE

This is a simple game in which the last player to three-putt a green during the round of play has to pay everyone else a predetermined amount of money. If two players both three-putt the last green then the player that last putted for his or her three-putt has the Snake and pays everyone else. Lagging for that two-putt is really important here, especially if someone else already has the Snake!

SNAKES

This is the same type of game as Snake, but in this game anyone who three-putts a green pays the other players in the foursome whatever amount has been decided before play. This type of game will either provide you with the monetary incentive to pay more attention to your putting and improve it or result in your developing the "yip" malady.

WALK WALK

This is a game played in the Northwest (Washington and Oregon), in which any player can challenge another player who is about to putt by saying he or she will three-putt the green. If the challenged player sinks the putt for a one-putt then the challenger loses the bet. If the challenged player takes two putts to hole out then there is no winner—the bet is a push. If, however, the challenged player three-putts the green, then that player loses the bet.

If you play this game for $5, $10, or even higher stakes, don't be surprised when players' sphincter muscles really tighten up! Good players suddenly lose their putting touch, and you learn what pressure is and realize to a certain extent how a pro feels when faced with a three-foot putt to win top prize money.

TEE GAME

On the first tee you and your partner flip a coin or tee with your opponents to see who wins the honors to tee off first. The team that tees off first must hold the tee with their best ball; if they do they win 1 point apiece, and if they lose the tee box honors they lose 3 points apiece. In this game a tie for best ball results in a push and the team that held the tee box maintains honors on the next tee, with no points awarded. Thus each team that has the tee box honors has the chance to either win a point or lose 3 points on each hole. The players I know who play this game usually play for either 50 cents or $1 per point.

RABBIT

This game is played by three or more players and requires that the winner win four legs. Every player antes into the pot a prearranged amount and the winner takes all. In order to win, a player must win four holes outright from all the other players. A tie score does not count as a win. In this game carryovers do not count. Four individual holes must be won in order for a player to win the pot. The first player to win four holes without having another player tie or beat his or her score is the winner.

RABBITS

This is the same game as Rabbit, except that if a player does win four legs then another game of Rabbit, with the same stakes, is automatically started. In the event that no player wins four legs after the completion of 18 holes and if you are not going to play 27, then the player with the most legs wins the pot, unless it's been decided otherwise prior to playing.

TICKS

This is a game played in Canada, and possibly elsewhere, in which players are awarded a point, or points, on each hole for accomplishing one or more of the following: 1 point for long drive in the fairway, 1 point for being first on the green, 1 point for being closest to the pin once all players are on the green, and 1 point for being the first player to hole out.

As might be noted, this game is somewhat similar to other point games, especially Bingo-Bango-Bongo. In this game, as in the other games, just add everyone's points at the end of the round. The winner is the

> *"Nothing comes down slower than a golf handicap."*
> —Bobby Nichols, *Never Say Never*, 1965

player with the highest point total and is paid by the other players based upon the point differentials.

TWENTY-ONE

This is a putting game with two or more players with the first player to achieve 21 points being the winner. Points are achieved as follows: A one-putt earns 3 points, and being closest to the hole if there is no one-putt earns 1 point. If no putt has been made after everyone has putted twice, then the ball closest to the hole earns 2 points. Point differentials decide how much the winner collects from the other players. If it's been decided beforehand and three or more players are involved, then all places can be paid based on point differentials.

UMBRELLA

This is a team game of additional side bets. In this game a total of 6 points are up for grabs and are earned as follows: 1 point for being closest to the pin in regulation, 1 point for the low ball, 1 point for the fewest combined putts, 1 point for a birdie, and 2 points for the low team score. No points are won or lost in the case of ties. If a team wins all 6 points on a hole it is called an Umbrella, and in that event all points are doubled so that the losing team on the hole loses 12 points.

> *"There is no such individual as a born golfer."*
> —Ben Hogan

THE SIDE GAMES WE PLAY & WAGER: GROUP TWO

In this chapter some of the basic individual and team games are covered as well as some of the offshoots of those games. Games such as Medal Play, Match Play, and Nassau are explained, as are some of the variations of those games.

These games usually involve the cumulative performance of a player for a round of golf rather than specific aspects of golf as covered in Group One. Some of the games, with or without a partner, might involve only nine or six holes before partners are changed or a new game is started. Additionally, with some of the games you will find that even though you didn't play in the same group with a player or players you can still arrange a bet with that longtime rival or rivals!

MEDAL PLAY or STROKE PLAY
MEDAL PLAY HANDICAP
MATCH PLAY
MATCH PLAY HANDICAP
NASSAU
PRESS or ROLL THE DRUMS
NASSAU—PARTNERS
NASSAU—PARTNERS—LOW BALL, LOW TOTAL
NASSAU—PARTNERS—LOW BALL, HIGH BALL
NASSAU FOUR WAYS
NASSAU SIX WAYS
ROBBINS or SIXES or SIX-HOLE SWITCH
ROBBINS NASSAU
STABLEFORD
BRITISH STABLEFORD

JOKER STABLEFORD
THREESOME SIX-POINT GAME
EAST COAST POINT GAME
CHAIRMAN
PARROT
COYOTE KILL
HOGAN POINT GAME
AUSTRALIAN HOGAN
POINT GAME
SEVEN-POINT GAME
POINT A HOLE
LOW NET FOURSOME
PER YARD PER HOLE or YARDAGES
BLIND-DRAW BEST BALL
BOGEY
DOUBLE BOGEY or DBs

MEDAL PLAY or STROKE PLAY

This is one of the basic forms of play in golf for both the professional and the amateur. It is simply the total number of strokes a player requires to complete a round of golf versus the opponents and their total strokes. Very simply, the low score wins. You just play for a set amount of money for the 18 holes, whether it be $1 or $100. A variation holds that if there is a stroke differential between players, that stroke differential is multiplied by an agreed-upon amount, with the high-score player paying this amount to the low-score player.

For instance, Player A and Player B are playing for $5 per stroke differential. Player A shoots an 86 while Player B shoots an 82. Based upon their bet, Player A pays Player B $20. If the members of your foursome have the same level of playing ability, you can usually have individual games with the other players using the same format as above. Even though all four players might have handicaps (which indicate their level of playing ability) within a shot or two of each other, I can just about guarantee that the final scores of all players will show more than just a shot or two difference. Sometimes it just boils down to who's hot and who's not! (See scorecard example 2-1.)

MEDAL PLAY HANDICAP

This is similar to Medal Play, but handicaps are used to bring some parity to players who don't play at the same level of proficiency. In this game a player's handicap is subtracted from the gross score to result in a

MEDAL PLAY or STROKE PLAY
Scorecard 2-1

HOLE	1	2	3	4	5	6	7	8	9	Out
Black Tees	422	347	107	598	392	239	454	517	414	3490
Gold Tees	386	336	104	512	361	230	416	474	364	3183
Silver Tees	353	272	67	486	329	188	370	447	350	2862
PAR	4	4	3	5	4	3	4	5	4	36
Handicap	7	15	17	3	11	9	1	5	13	
PLAYER A (14)	5	5	3	5	6	5	5	5	5	44
PLAYER B (12)	5	4	3	6	5	3	4	5	4	39

In this Straight Medal Play or Stroke Play game, Player B wins by four shots.

INITIALS	10	11	12	13	14	15	16	17	18	In	Tot	Hcp	Net
	362	445	548	324	183	435	169	403	589	3458	6948		
	337	406	509	281	150	413	139	374	564	3173	6356		
	326	377	443	255	95	335	116	349	503	2799	5661		
	4	4	5	4	3	4	3	4	5	36	72		
	16	6	4	12	14	2	18	8	10				
A	5	4	5	6	3	5	4	4	6	42	86		
B	5	5	7	3	3	4	4	6	6	43	82		

net score that is compared with the net score of the other player. If you are playing partners then you can either bet the low net best ball of the partners versus that of your opponents or the net total score of the partners versus that of your opponents. As in straight Medal Play, you can bet a set amount of money for the low net score or have a bet based upon the stroke differential of the scores. In either case, when playing partners, both partners pay off the bet.

MATCH PLAY

This game is played hole by hole and the winner of each hole is the player with the lowest score on that hole. Each hole won counts as a plus, while a hole lost counts as a minus. A hole that is tied is halved. The player at the end of the round of golf that has the most holes won after subtracting the holes lost is the winner. In this game your total gross score, which might be lower than your opponent's, does not necessarily mean you're going to win. I've shot an 82 and lost to a player who shot an 88. It just so happens that the player with the 88 had three bad holes (we are talking about triple-bogey-type bad holes), while the rest of the round was more than respectable. You bet this game the same way or ways that you do in Medal Play with or without a partner. (See scorecard example 2-2.)

"Stroke play is a better test of golf, but match play is a better test of character."
                                        —Joe Carr, Irish amateur

MATCH PLAY HANDICAP

This is the same game as straight Match Play with the exception that handicaps are used. There are a few ways to handle the handicap, but the most common method involves the player with the lower handicap allowing the player with the higher handicap to deduct a stroke from the gross score achieved on a number of holes equal to the difference between their handicaps. For example, if the difference between the handicaps is 5, then the high-handicap player would take a stroke on the first five handicap stroke holes, as indicated on scorecard example 2-2. Remember that the handicap stroke holes are not in order on the scorecard, but rather are indicated 1 through 18 based upon each hole's level of difficulty. You should also note that the odd-numbered stroke holes are on the first nine holes and the even-numbered stroke holes on the back side or second nine holes. The handicap stroke hole indicated as 1 is supposed to be the most difficult hole to play on the course. The stroke holes are intended to be an equalizer between players of differing handicaps, but be cautious of the sandbagger with an inflated handicap!

Another way in which the game can be played is to have both players take their full handicaps wherever they fall on the scorecard, with the low score, regardless of whether it is a gross or a net score, winning that hole. In this game, as in others, you can bet a set amount for whoever wins the most holes or you can wager a set amount multiplied by the number of holes the winner wins by. This game can be and often is played with partners; the format and the betting are the same for a singles match. Remember that if you are

MATCH AND NASSAU GAMES
Scorecard 2-2

HOLE	1	2	3	4	5	6	7	8	9	Out
Black Tees	422	347	107	598	392	239	454	517	414	3490
Gold Tees	386	336	104	512	361	230	416	474	364	3183
Silver Tees	353	272	67	486	329	188	370	447	350	2862
PAR	4	4	3	5	4	3	4	5	4	36
Handicap	7	15	17	3	11	9	1	5	13	
PLAYER A (14)	5	5	3	5	6	5	⑤	5	5	44
PLAYER B (12)	5	4	3	6	5	3	4	5	4	39
MATCH	-	-1	-1	-	-1	-2	-2	-2	-3	
NASSAU	-	-1	-1	-	-1	-2	-2	-2	-3	-3

As indicated here, Player A gets two shots from Player B because of the handicap differential (shot holes circled). Scoring is from Player A's standpoint.

INITIALS	10	11	12	13	14	15	16	17	18	In	Tot	Hcp	Net
	362	445	548	324	183	435	169	403	589	3458	6948		
	337	406	509	281	150	413	139	374	564	3173	6356		
	326	377	443	255	95	335	116	349	503	2799	5661		
	4	4	5	4	3	4	3	4	5	36	72		
	16	6	4	12	14	2	18	8	10				
A	5	4	5	6	3	⑤	4	4	6	42	86		
B	5	5	7	3	3	4	4	6	6	43	82		
	-3	-2	-1	-2	-2	-2	-2	-1	-1		-1		
	-	+1	+2	+1	+1	+1	+1	+2	+2	+2	-1		

Here, in the Match Play game, Player A loses by one hole to Player B. In the Nassau game, Player A loses the front side −3 but wins the back side +2. Player A therefore loses the total Nassau −1 and loses one bet.

playing partners, both players pay the prearranged bet to the winning players.

NASSAU

This is probably the most common game and the one golfers are most familiar with. The game is basically three matches with the front nine holes constituting one match, the back nine holes another, and the 18-hole total making the third match. So, if a player is playing a $2 Nassau, the front side is played for $2, the back side is played for $2, and the total is worth $2.

In a Nassau bet each hole is played as an individual match so that a player who scores a par 4 to beat an opponent who shot a 5 goes 1 up. On the next hole, if the player who shot a par 4 on the first hole scores a bogey 5 but still beats the opponent who shot a double bogey, the first player goes 2 up. If both players on the third hole shoot bogeys, there is no blood and the player who shot the par 4 on the first hole still remains 2 up (or +2). The match is played in this manner for the first nine holes, and whoever is up at that point wins the front side.

The back nine holes are played the same way, but the players start a new match on the 10th hole. Whoever wins the 10th hole goes 1 up (or +1). Once again, whoever is up after playing the back nine wins that side. If both players come out even then that side is a push and no one wins. However, let's say that the player who shot that par 4 on the first hole wins the front side by +3 and that the player lost the back side to the opponent by −2. In this case the player would win the total by +1. In the event that our players each win a side by +3, then they played all day for a tie. No one wins.

This game can become more interesting with the introduction of presses. A press occurs when a player who is losing starts another bet hoping to offset the one he or she is losing, or possibly to bring the first bet to even and win the press bet to win that side. A press bet is just another bet, like the one in progress, but it starts at whichever hole the player requests. In most cases, a press bet is initiated once a player is 2 down.

As an example, let's say that our press player is 2 down after two holes and on the third tee presses his opponent. Our player then wins the third hole, and as a result his bet status is 1 down on the original bet and 1 up on the press bet. Let's say that our press player then wins the fourth hole and therefore goes to even on the original bet and 2 up on his press bet. However, now his opponent is down 2 on the press bet and therefore decides to press the press bet, which is perfectly legal. So with this new scenario, let's say that our press player loses the fifth hole after winning two holes, and so goes to −1 on the original bet, 1 up on his press bet, and now 1 down on his opponent's press bet. Let's say that the nine holes end with our press player losing the original bet down 2, winning his press bet +1, and losing on his opponent's press bct 2 down. Our press player would therefore lose one bet since his press bet negated one of his opponent's bets.

> *"The mind messes up more shots than the body."*
> —Tommy Bolt

In this game it doesn't matter if one of the bets is won by 4 or 5 up; it can still be negated and result in a push even if another bet is only won by 1 up. In a Nassau bet you can have as many presses as are accepted; however, only the original bet will count to the total after you have played 18 holes.

Additionally, this is a game that can be played not only by two players but also by a threesome, and in more cases than not by a foursome. In the case of a threesome, each player can have an individual Nassau game with the other two players. In the case of a foursome, the players can either play individual matches among themselves or play a team match coupled with individual matches. The team matches and their various formats are described next in this chapter. (See scorecard example 2-2.)

PRESS or ROLL THE DRUMS

This is a bet made during a match in addition to the original bet and is made by the player or team that is losing. The press bet, which in the majority of cases involves a Nassau match or a variation of the Nassau, runs only for the holes remaining to be played on either the front nine holes or the back nine holes at the point that the press bet was declared. In most cases a press bet is called when a player or team is at least 2 down. The player or team that is ahead does

> *"You don't know what pressure is until you play for five bucks with only two in your pocket."*
> —Lee Trevino, *Newsweek*, 1971

not have to accept the press; however, it is customary and traditional to accept it. Though local rules vary, press bets have been called when anyone is angry, meaning press at anytime, or a press bet must be called on the hole where a player or team goes 2 down. Other local rules call for automatic press bets when a player or team goes 2 down on any bet, whether it is the original bet or a subsequent press bet.

NASSAU—PARTNERS

This game is played with the same format as Nassau but with a partner. I've played this game several ways, one of which is just best ball of the partners versus that of your opponents. Another way to play is with each hole worth 2 points, 1 point for low ball and 1 point for low total. If there is a tie for low ball between the teams, the hole is halved for the low ball point. If there is also a tie for low total between the teams, this point is also halved and no points are won or lost. This is a good game because it keeps everyone in the match. As an example, you shoot a triple-bogey 7 while your partner gets a birdie 3 and your opponents both shoot bogey 5s. In this case you and your partner would win 1 point for low ball and push with your opponents for low total since you both had 10s. Press bets are played the same way they are played in an individual Nassau match. (See scorecard example 2-3.)

NASSAU—PARTNERS—LOW BALL, LOW TOTAL

This is another variation of the Nassau that you play with a partner. In this game low ball is played as an individual match between the teams, and so is the low total. Going back to the previous example above—where you shot the triple-bogey 7, your partner shot the birdie 3, and your opponents both shot 5s—in this game, your team would be +1 on the low ball match and even on the low total match. If on the next hole you and your partner shoot par 4s while your opponents again shoot bogey 5s, you win both the low ball and the low total. You would now be +2 on the low ball match and +1 on the low total match. Press bets are handled the same as in a straight Nassau game. In this example, the team that was down 2 on the low ball match could press if they desired. (See scorecard example 2-4.)

NASSAU—PARTNERS—LOW BALL, HIGH BALL

This is just another variation on the previous game, but in this case the team that has the individual high ball loses a point. As in the example under "Nassau—Partners"—where you shot the 7 and your partner shot the 3 while each of your opponents shot a 5—in this game you win a point for the low ball and lose a point for having the high score (the 7). If you are playing 2 points a hole and not having separate team matches for low ball or high ball, then your match would be even. If, on the other hand, you are having separate matches, then your team would be +1 for the low ball

NASSAU GAME

Scorecard 2-3

HOLE	1	2	3	4	5	6	7	8	9	Out
Black Tees	422	347	107	598	392	239	454	517	414	3490
Gold Tees	386	336	104	512	361	230	416	474	364	3183
Silver Tees	353	272	67	486	329	188	370	447	350	2862
PAR	4	4	3	5	4	3	4	5	4	36
Handicap	7	15	17	3	11	9	1	5	13	
PLAYER A (12)	5	4	3	6	5	3	4	5	4	39
PLAYER B (14)	5	5	3	5	6	5	5	5	5	44
PLAYER C (11)	4	4	3	6	4	3	5	5	5	39
PLAYER D (15)	6	5	4	7	6	4	5	6	4	47
LOW BALL/LOW TOT.	-1	-1	0	+2	0	-1	+1	+2	+2	+2
LOW BALL/HIGH BALL	-	-	+1	+3	+2	+1	+2	+3	+3	+3

Low Ball, Low Total and Low Ball, High Ball with Player A with a 12 handicap and Player B with a 14 handicap versus Player C with an 11 handicap and Player D with a 15 handicap. Teams will play even since total handicaps of both teams equal 26. Scoring is from Team AB's standpoint.

INITIALS	10	11	12	13	14	15	16	17	18	In	Tot	Hcp	Net
	362	445	548	324	183	435	169	403	589	3458	6948		
	337	406	509	281	150	413	139	374	564	3173	6356		
	326	377	443	255	95	335	116	349	503	2799	5661		
	4	4	5	4	3	4	3	4	5	36	72		
	16	6	4	12	14	2	18	8	10				
A	5	5	7	3	3	4	4	6	6	43	82		
B	5	4	5	6	3	5	4	4	6	42	86		
C	4	5	6	5	3	4	4	3	6	40	79		
D	5	5	6	5	3	5	5	6	5	45	92		
	-2	-	+1	+3	+3	+3	+4	+2	-	-	+2		
	-1	-	-	-	-	-	+1	-	-1	-1	+2		

In this example, Team AB in the Low Ball, Low Total match win the front side, tie the back side, and win the total match +2. Team AB therefore wins two bets. In the Low Ball, High Ball match, Team AB wins the front side +3 but loses the back side −1. Therefore they win the total match +2. Team AB wins one bet.

and −1 for the high ball. Press bets are handled the same way as in the previous Nassau examples. (See scorecard example 2-4.)

NASSAU FOUR WAYS

The format for this game is the same as for a normal Nassau bet, except that the back side counts for two bets. As an example, if you or your team is playing a $2 Nassau, the front side will count $2, the back side will count $4, and the total 18 will count $2. Therefore you or your team can conceivably win a total of $8 for the match.

NASSAU SIX WAYS

In this variation on the Nassau bet, the front side counts as one bet, the back side counts as two bets, and the total for the 18 counts as three bets. The reasoning for this type of Nassau is that if a player or team beats the opponents on the front side by 3 or 4 up but loses the back side by 1 or 2, they should at least win something—which would not be the case in a Nassau Four Ways. In the case of a $2 match a player or team can conceivably win $12 for the match.

> *"We're not trying to humiliate the greatest players in the world. We're trying to identify them."*
> —Frank Tatum, *Sports Illustrated,* 1984, on the tough conditions of U.S. Open courses

ROBBINS or SIXES or SIX-HOLE SWITCH

These are all names that Texans use to describe a foursome in which you change partners after every six holes. This allows you to play with everyone as a partner at some point. Partners are usually decided by a ball toss or by one player flipping a tee and the partner being chosen by whoever the tip of the tee is pointing to. I've played this game several ways: a straight best ball of the partners; low ball, low total; or total score of the partners. You can bet on the winner of the six-hole match or bet a set amount times the point or score differential between the teams. Usually Robbins is played while other individual games are being played.

ROBBINS NASSAU

This is played the same way as a Robbins game, except that you break up each six-hole match into a Nassau bet, with the first three holes being the front side and the last three holes being the back side, and then figure the total for the six holes. This is done for each six-hole match that you play with a different partner. This game is bet the same as you would a regular 18-hole Nassau match and can be played as a best ball, a low ball, low total, or a total score of the partners.

> *"Golf is a good walk spoiled."*
> —Mark Twain

NASSAU GAMES

Scorecard 2-4

HOLE	1	2	3	4	5	6	7	8	9	Out
Black Tees	422	347	107	598	392	239	454	517	414	3490
Gold Tees	386	336	104	512	361	230	416	474	364	3183
Silver Tees	353	272	67	486	329	188	370	447	350	2862
PAR	4	4	3	5	4	3	4	5	4	36
Handicap	7	15	17	3	11	9	1	5	13	
PLAYER A (12)	5	4	3	6	5	3	4	5	4	39
B (14)	5	5	3	5	6	5	5	5	5	44
PLAYER C (11)	4	4	3	6	4	3	5	5	5	39
D (15)	6	5	4	7	6	4	5	6	4	47
LOW BALL	-1	-1	-1	-	-1	-1	-	-	-	-
LOW TOTAL	-	-	+1	+2	+1 / -1	- / -2	+1 / -1	+2 / -	+2 / -	+2 / -
LOW BALL	-1	-1	-1	-	-1	-1	-	-	-	-
HIGH BALL	+1	+1	+2	+3 / +1	+3 / +1	+2 / -	+2 / -	+3 / +1	+3 / +1	+3 / +1

The Low Ball, Low Total and the Low Ball, High Ball matches are played as a separate Nassau game with automatic presses when 2 down, as illustrated here. The teams are Players AB versus Players CD with the scoring from Team AB's standpoint.

In this example, Players AB break even in the Low Ball but lose the press bet, so they lose one bet. In the Low Total game, Players AB win the front +2, tie the back, and win the overall +2 but lose one press bet.

INITIALS	10	11	12	13	14	15	16	17	18	In	Tot	Hcp	Net
	362	445	548	324	183	435	169	403	589	3458	6948		
	337	406	509	281	150	413	139	374	564	3173	6356		
	326	377	443	255	95	335	116	349	503	2799	5661		
	4	4	5	4	3	4	3	4	5	36	72		
	16	6	4	12	14	2	18	8	10				
A	5	5	7	3	3	4	4	6	6	43	82		
B	5	4	5	6	3	5	4	4	6	42	86		
C	4	5	6	5	3	4	4	3	6	40	79		
D	5	5	6	5	3	5	5	6	5	45	92		
LB	-1	-	+1	+2	+2	+2	+2	+1/-1	-2	-2	-		
LT	-1	-	-	+1	+1	+1	+2	+1/-1	-2	-2	+2		
LB	-1	-	+1	+2	+2	+2	+2	+1/-1	-2	-2	-		
HB	-	-	-1	-2	-2	-2	-1/+1	-1/+1	-1/+1	-1/+1	+2		

Therefore Team AB wins one bet. Overall in the Low Ball, Low Total games, the teams would break even.

Players AB in the High Ball game win the front +3 and a press +1, lose the back side −1, but win the total +2 and win a press bet. Therefore Players AB in the High Ball game would win three bets. Overall in the Low Ball, High Ball games, Team AB would win a total of two bets.

STABLEFORD

In Stableford, you play against everyone else. The game is based on a point system in which a player wins or loses points as determined by score. The points are determined as follows: 8 points for a double eagle, 5 for an eagle, 2 for a birdie, 0 for a par, −1 for a bogey, and −3 for a double bogey or worse. Since the majority of golfers are not professionals, this game is usually played with golfers using their full handicaps to arrive at a net score from which they determine their point awards, either positive or negative. The value of a point is whatever everyone agrees to, whether 10 cents or $1 per point. The winner is the player who, at the end of 18 holes, has more points than any other player. The other players pay the winner the difference in their point totals from the winner's point total multiplied by the value of each point. You can also play that third place pays off second place and that fourth place pays off both second and third place. If you decide to play the latter, fourth place could prove to be expensive, since you pay everyone! Have the other three pay for drinks! (See scorecard example 2-5.)

BRITISH STABLEFORD

In another Stableford game played primarily in Britain, points are awarded to players based upon the following: 1 point for a bogey, 2 points for a par, 3 points for a birdie, and 4 points for an eagle. This game can be played with full handicaps, and the player who earns the most points wins.

STABLEFORD
Scorecard 2-5

HOLE	1	2	3	4	5	6	7	8	9	Out
Black Tees	422	347	107	598	392	239	454	517	414	3490
Gold Tees	386	336	104	512	361	230	416	474	364	3183
Silver Tees	353	272	67	486	329	188	370	447	350	2862
PAR	4	4	3	5	4	3	4	5	4	36
Handicap	7	15	17	3	11	9	1	5	13	
PLAYER A (12)	⑤	4	3	⑥	⑤	③	④	⑤	4	39
	0	0	0	0	0	2	2	2	0	6 PTS.
B (14)	⑤	5	3	⑤	⑥	⑤	⑤	⑤	⑤	44
	0	-1	0	2	-1	-1	0	2	0	1 PT.
C (11)	④	4	3	⑥	④	③	⑤	⑤	5	39
	2	0	0	0	2	2	0	2	-1	7 PTS.
D (15)	⑥	⑤	4	⑦	⑥	④	⑤	⑥	④	47
	-1	0	-1	-1	-1	0	0	0	2	-2 PTS.

This is a game with players getting full handicaps (handicap holes are circled), with points earned or lost on each hole as indicated below each player's score.

INITIALS	10	11	12	13	14	15	16	17	18	In	Tot	Hcp	Net
	362	445	548	324	183	435	169	403	589	3458	6948		
	337	406	509	281	150	413	139	374	564	3173	6356		
	326	377	443	255	95	335	116	349	503	2799	5661		
	4	4	5	4	3	4	3	4	5	36	72		
	16	6	4	12	14	2	18	8	10				
A	5	⑤	⑦	③	3	④	4	⑥	⑥	43	82		
	-1	0	-1	5	0	2	-1	-1	0	3 PTS	9 PTS. TOTAL		
B	5	④	⑤	⑥	③	⑤	4	④	⑥	42	86		
	-1	2	2	-1	2	0	-1	2	0	5 PTS	6 PTS TOTAL		
C	4	⑤	⑥	5	3	④	4	③	⑥	40	79		
	0	0	0	-1	0	2	-1	5	0	5 PTS	12 PTS TOTAL		
D	5	⑤	⑥	⑤	③	⑤	5	⑥	⑤	45	92		
	-1	0	0	0	2	0	-3	-1	2	-1 PT.	-3 PTS. TOTAL		

In this particular game, Player C would win 3 points from Player A, 6 points from Player B, and 15 points from Player D. If you were to play a team Stableford with AB versus CD, then Team AB would win 6 points from Team CD (15 points total for Team AB minus 9 points total for Team CD).

JOKER STABLEFORD

This game is played in Spain and uses the same format as the Stableford previously explained, with the one exception that each player is allowed to declare, prior to teeing off, one hole on the front side and one hole on the back side as a Joker hole. The player who declares a hole a Joker hole gets whatever points were earned for that hole doubled. If two or more players use the same hole as a Joker hole, then the points earned by each individual player who declared the hole a Joker hole are doubled. The player with the most points at the end of the round is the winner and is paid by the other players based upon the point differentials.

THREESOME SIX-POINT GAME

With this threesome format each player has 2 points to protect on each hole. The game is a best ball and may be played with handicaps. Each player plays the other two players for a point each. Thus if Player A beats Players B and C, Player A retains 2 points for the hole but also wins 1 point from Player B and 1 from Player C to win a total of 4 points on the hole. If Player B beats Player C, then Player B retains 1 point and wins 1 point from Player C, for a total of 2 points on the hole. Player C ends up with 0 points on the hole.

The total is always 6 points, and the most any single player can win on one hole is 4 points. No points are won or traded on ties. Add up all points at the end of play to see who owes what to whom. If you do not end up with at least 36 points (two times 18 holes), you

will be a loser. Sometimes there is one winner, sometimes two, but never three!

EAST COAST POINT GAME

This is another point game played primarily on the
East Coast of the United States. It can be played by
two, three, or four players—and conceivably more. In
this game, played with full handicaps, players can
earn points on each hole based upon the following
format: 5 points for an eagle, 3 points for a birdie, 2
points for a par, and 1 point for a bogey. Each player
on each hole is in essence playing against himself or
herself. As in some other games described in this and
other chapters, a player is not concerned about playing in comparison to the other players but rather
about playing in comparison to par. The winner in
this game is the player who has achieved the highest
point total for the 18 holes. The winner is then paid by
the other players based upon point differentials. The
dollar value of each point is decided prior to playing
the round.

> *"Watching Sam Snead practice hitting golf balls is
> like watching a fish practice swimming."*
> —John Schlee, *Golf Digest,* 1977

CHAIRMAN

This is another threesome game, one in which the first player to win a hole regardless of score, using full handicaps and without being tied, becomes the Chairman and "assumes the chair." If the Chairman wins the next hole, then he or she wins a point from the two other players. If the Chairman is tied on a hole, no points are lost or won and the Chairman retains the chair. If one of the other two players wins a hole then he or she becomes the Chairman, but no points are lost or won. Therefore, it becomes obvious that in order to win points, a player has to win two holes, possibly separated by holes that might have been tied, before money is won or lost. (See scorecard example 2-6.)

PARROT

This is the same game as Chairman. However, instead of being in the chair if a player wins a hole outright, the player is said to be the Parrot and is now "on the perch." The point-earning system is the same as in Chairman.

COYOTE KILL

Coyote Kill is suitable for golfers who belong to a club or a group of eight or more golfers who get together to play every week or every other week. For this game each player antes a set amount into a common pot, whether $1 or $20 per player. The game to be played is

CHAIRMAN

Scorecard 2-6

HOLE	1	2	3	4	5	6	7	8	9	Out
Black Tees	422	347	107	598	392	239	454	517	414	3490
Gold Tees	386	336	104	512	361	230	416	474	364	3183
Silver Tees	353	272	67	486	329	188	370	447	350	2862
PAR	4	4	3	5	4	3	4	5	4	36
Handicap	7	15	17	3	11	9	1	5	13	
PLAYER A (15)	④	5̇	3	7̇	5̇	4	6̇	6̇	⑤	45
B (18)	5	6̇	4̇	6̇	5̇	5̇	5̇	7	6̇	49
C (23)	5̇	6̇	5̇	⑦	6̇	4̇	⑤̇	5̈	6̇	49

In this game players are playing with full handicaps (handicaps are in parentheses), with the shots due each player indicated by dots on the appropriate shot holes. A player who becomes Chairman is indicated by a circle.

As indicated here, Player A becomes the Chairman on hole 1 and wins 1 point. Player C becomes Chairman on hole 4 but wins no points. Player C assumes the chair on hole 7 and wins 1 point before losing the

INITIALS	10	11	12	13	14	15	16	17	18	In	Tot	Hcp	Net
	362	445	548	324	183	435	169	403	589	3458	6948		
	337	406	509	281	150	413	139	374	564	3173	6356		
	326	377	443	255	95	335	116	349	503	2799	5661		
	4	4	5	4	3	4	3	4	5	36	72		
	16	6	4	12	14	2	18	8	10				
A	4	5	5	4	5	6	4	(4)	6	43	88		
B	5	5	8	4	(3)	6	4	6	6	47	96		
C	6	5	6	4	4	(5)	3	6	6	45	94		

chair to Player A on hole 9. Player A retains the chair until hole 14 but wins no points. On hole 14 Player B assumes the chair but immediately loses such to Player C on hole 15. Player C as Chairman wins 1 point but loses the chair to Player A on hole 17. Player A wins no points since all players tie on hole 18. As a result, Player A wins no points for the game, Player B loses 3 points, and Player C wins 3 points.

determined by the previous winners after everyone has paid their antes. The games usually played are: Low Gross, Low Net (100 percent handicap), Skins (50 percent handicap), or Stableford (100 percent handicap). This game usually has at least 16 players, who use a deck of cards to determine partners. The two players who pull the same color ace, king, queen, or jack become partners—e.g., the two black aces are one team and the two red aces are another team. Regardless of the type of Coyote Kill that is played, this game involves having different players as partners and being involved in a variety of games.

HOGAN POINT GAME

This is played by a twosome, threesome, or foursome, with everyone playing alone or else playing this game in addition to any other game you arrange, such as a Nassau. This game simply awards 1 point to each player who hits the fairway on the drive, hits the green in regulation, or one- or two-putts, and 2 points for scoring a birdie. Point differences after 18 holes determine how much each player pays to the player with the highest point total. In some cases the low-total player and the second-low-total player pay off all other players.

AUSTRALIAN HOGAN

This is a point game for the more advanced player. Points are earned or lost based upon the following format: 1 point for hitting the fairway on your drive or

1 point lost for not hitting the fairway, 1 point for hitting the green in regulation or 1 point lost for not hitting the green in regulation, 2 points for a par, 3 points for a birdie, and 4 points for an eagle or better. On the other hand, 1 point is lost for a bogey, 2 points are lost for a double bogey, and 3 points are lost for anything over a double bogey. Once again, the point totals after 18 holes determine who pays whom.

POINT GAME

This game is very similar to Hogan, but points are awarded on the following basis: 1 point for a proxy (the ball closest to the hole), 2 points for a birdie, 1 point for the high ball, and 1 point for the low ball. The total possible points for a hole is 5. If there is a tie for the low or the high ball, no points are given. In this game even if a player is having a really bad hole, he or she can still win a point. Even with a score approaching double digits, the player can still possibly get 2 points for the hole, by not only having the high score but by also getting the proxy. The point totals after 18 holes determine who pays whom, once again based upon the point differentials of the players.

> *"The only shots you can be dead sure of are those you've had already."*
>
> —Byron Nelson

SEVEN-POINT GAME

In this game, one twosome plays against another two-some with the possibility of 7 points to be won on every hole. The points that can be won are as follows: 2 points for the twosome with the low ball of the foursome, 2 points for the twosome that does not have the high ball of the foursome, 1 point for a proxy in regulation, 1 point for a birdie, and 1 point for the twosome with the fewest total putts. In case of a tie, no points are won.

This game can be played using gross scores, providing that there is not a large discrepancy in handicaps between the twosomes. In most cases, however, this game is played with full handicaps so that net scores are used in determining the points won on each hole.

A Seven-Point Game also allows one press bet per nine holes, called a "knee bend." The knee bend, however, can be called only by the twosome that is down in points and is applicable only to hole number 9 and number 18. Also, if the knee bend is to be called it must be called on the 8th hole for the press on the 9th or on the 17th hole for the press on the 18th. If the knee bend is called, then all points are doubled in value for just the 9th hole or the 18th hole, or both. The winner is the twosome with the most points at the end of the round. Winnings are paid by each player of the losing twosome in an amount equal to the difference in point totals times the value of each point.

POINT A HOLE

This is a bet in which you play each hole for a predetermined point value and you play each hole as an individual match. At the end of 18 holes whoever has the most points wins. Winnings are determined by subtracting the point total from the other individual point totals multiplied by the value of the point.

LOW NET FOURSOME

If you have a good outing with three or four foursomes or more, this can be played in conjunction with other matches or bets. Everyone antes into a common pot and the winning foursome splits the pot. The game involves the total score of each foursome less the handicaps of each player in the foursome. The low net score wins the pot.

PER YARD PER HOLE or YARDAGES

I haven't heard of this game being played too often, but if the stakes are high, I imagine it could turn out to be quite expensive for a player or a team not playing very well. Very simply, it is a game in which you are betting on every hole and the bet on every hole is predetermined by the yardage of the hole. As an example, if the first hole is a par 4 of 400 yards, then the winner of the first hole wins 400 times whatever you are playing for. If you are playing for $1 per yard, then the player or team who wins the first hole wins $400.

If the average length of a golf course is approximately 6,000 yards, this type of game can prove to be costly.

BLIND-DRAW BEST BALL

This is a game played with eight or more players. Everyone places a set amount of money into the pot, whether 50 cents or $5, and then all the golfers play their regular game. After everyone has finished play, each player's name is placed in a hat and twosomes are drawn out to form the blind-draw twosomes. The twosome's best ball net score (full handicap strokes taken where indicated on the scorecard) on each hole is determined for the 18 holes and the winner is the twosome with the lowest score. With 12 or more players we usually pay three places.

> *"I never played a round when I didn't learn something new about the game."*
>
> —Ben Hogan

BOGEY

Lee Trevino supposedly played Bogey prior to playing on the professional tour. This game is usually played by golfers with a high level of proficiency, or low handicaps. The first player in the foursome to shoot a bogey or worse without another player scoring a bogey or worse on the hole pays a set amount to the other players. Play continues until each individual player shoots a bogey or worse. So if Player A scores a bogey on the first hole and all other players par the hole, then Player A pays. If Player B in the foursome shoots a bogey on the second hole, then B gets paid by A only for the first hole. If Player C bogeys the sixth hole, then C would be paid five times the agreed-upon amount. If Player D shoots a par round of golf, then Player D receives from Player A 18 times the agreed amount. If everyone gets a bogey or worse prior to the finish of 18 holes, after the last player has been paid, the foursome starts another game, which is played the same way.

The Bogey game also works with players utilizing their full handicaps and taking their shots where they fall on the scorecard. Once again, the player who first scores a bogey or worse whether it be a gross or a net bogey, without another player scoring a bogey or worse pays each of the players the agreed-upon amount on each hole played until each player finally scores a bogey or worse. (See scorecard example 2-7.)

DOUBLE BOGEY or DBs

This game is an offshoot of Bogey and is probably more suited for players who do not have low handicaps. In this game, with or without handicaps, the player who first shoots a double bogey or worse without another player doing so pays the other players an agreed-upon amount on each hole that is played until each of the players scores a double bogey or worse. Once all players have scored a double bogey or worse, another game can be started for the balance of the holes to be played. Remember that in this game the player who first shoots the double bogey pays each player on each hole played until the player shoots a double bogey or worse. Another game is not started until the last player in the foursome has shot that double bogey. This is a game that can be played for 10 cents a hole or $10 a hole. (See scorecard example 2-8.)

"As of this writing, there are approximately 2,450 reasons why a person hits a rotten shot and more are being discovered every day."
                    —Jay Cronley, *Playboy,* 1981

BOGEY GAME
Scorecard 2-7

HOLE	1	2	3	4	5	6	7	8	9	Out
Black Tees	422	347	107	598	392	239	454	517	414	3490
Gold Tees	386	336	104	512	361	230	416	474	364	3183
Silver Tees	353	272	67	486	329	188	370	447	350	2862
PAR	4	4	3	5	4	3	4	5	4	36
Handicap	7	15	17	3	11	9	1	5	13	
PLAYER A (6)	4	4	2	6	4	3	5	⑥	4	38
B (4)	4	3	3	5	4	3	5	5	5	37
C (5)	⑤	4	3	6	4	3	6	5	4	40
D (7)	4	4	3	5	5	3	4	5	6	39

In this scorecard example, the players are playing gross score. The Bogey players who pay are circled and the players who score a subsequent bogey are underlined. In this example, four Bogey games are played through 18 holes.

In this sample game, Player C becomes the first Bogey player (hole 1) and therefore loses 3 points to Player A (bogey on hole 4), loses 6 points to Player B (bogey on hole 7), and loses 4 points to Player D (bogey on hole 5). Player A becomes the next Bogey player (hole 8) and loses 1 point to Player B (bogey on hole 9), loses 3 points to Player C (bogey on hole 11), and loses 1 point to Player D (bogey on hole 9).

INITIALS	10	11	12	13	14	15	16	17	18	In	Tot	Hcp	Net
	362	445	548	324	183	435	169	403	589	3458	6948		
	337	406	509	281	150	413	139	374	564	3173	6356		
	326	377	443	255	95	335	116	349	503	2799	5661		
	4	4	5	4	3	4	3	4	5	36	72		
	16	6	4	12	14	2	18	8	10				
	5	5	5	4	3	6	3	5	5	41	79		
	4	4	⑥	3	3	5	④	4	5	38	75		
	4	5	5	4	2	6	3	5	5	39	79		
	4	4	⑥	5	3	4	3	4	5	38	77		

The next Bogey players are Players B and D (hole 12), who both lose 3 points to Player A (bogey on hole 15) and lose 3 points to Player C (bogey on hole 15). The next Bogey player is Player B (hole 16), who loses 1 point to Player A (bogey on hole 17), loses 1 point to Player C (bogey on hole 17), and loses 3 points to Player D.

Results of this game are as follows:

Player A: $+ 3 - 5 + 6 + 1$ = 5 total points won
Player B: $+ 6 + 1 - 6 - 5$ = 4 total points lost
Player C: $- 13 + 3 + 6 + 1$ = 3 total points lost
Player D: $+ 4 + 1 - 6 + 3$ = 2 total points won

DOUBLE-BOGEY GAME
Scorecard 2-8

HOLE	1	2	3	4	5	6	7	8	9	Out
Black Tees	422	347	107	598	392	239	454	517	414	3490
Gold Tees	386	336	104	512	361	230	416	474	364	3183
Silver Tees	353	272	67	486	329	188	370	447	350	2862
PAR	4	4	3	5	4	3	4	5	4	36
Handicap	7	15	17	3	11	9	1	5	13	
PLAYER A (25)	5	6	4	7	5	4	6	5	7	49
B (23)	(6)	5	4	6	(6)	5	6	6	6	50
C (24)	5	5	3	8	5	5	6	5	6	48
D (25)	4	5	4	7	(6)	4	5	(7)	5	47

The players in this scorecard example are playing gross scores. The Double-Bogey players that lose points are circled and the other players who subsequently score a double bogey are underlined. In this example, six games are played through 18 holes.

In this sample Double-Bogey game, Player B becomes the first Double-Bogey player (DB) (hole 1) and loses 1 point to Player A (DB on hole 2) loses 3 points to Player C (DB on hole 4), and loses 3 points to Player D (DB on hole 4). Players B and D, the next DB players, lose 2 points to Player A (DB on hole 7) and lose 1 point to Player C (DB on hole 6). Player D, the next DB player, loses 1 point to Player A, 1 point to Player B, and 1 point to Player C. Player C, the next DB player, loses 1 point to Player A, 2 points to Player B,

INITIALS	10	11	12	13	14	15	16	17	18	In	Tot	Hcp	Net
	362	445	548	324	183	435	169	403	589	3458	6948		
	337	406	509	281	150	413	139	374	564	3173	6356		
	326	377	443	255	95	335	116	349	503	2799	5661		
	4	4	5	4	3	4	3	4	5	36	72		
	16	6	4	12	14	2	18	8	10				
A	5	6	6	4	4	(6)	4	(6)	7	48	97	25	72
B	4	5	7	5	3	5	5	(6)	6	46	96	23	73
C	(6)	5	7	4	4	(6)	4	(6)	6	48	96	24	72
D	5	7	6	5	4	(6)	4	5	6	48	95	25	70

and 1 point to Player D. Players A, C, and D become the next DB players, and they each lose 1 point to Player B. Players A, B, and C are the last DB players, and they each lose 2 points to Player D.

Results of this game are as follows:

Player A: $+ 1 + 4 + 1 + 1 - 1 - 2$ = 4 total points won

Player B: $- 7 - 3 + 1 + 2 + 3 - 2$ = 6 total points lost

Player C: $+ 3 + 2 + 1 - 4 - 1 - 2$ = 1 total point lost

Player D: $+ 3 - 3 - 3 + 1 - 1 + 6$ = 3 total points won

TRIVIA:
MAKING THE TURN!

▷ The first "Open (British) Championship" was held in 1860 at the Prestwick Club in Scotland and had eight participants.

▷ The first United States Open championship was held in 1895.

▷ Golf got started in the United States in 1888, in Yonkers, New York.

▷ The most expensive country club in the world is in Japan. Membership at the Koganei Country Club, Tokyo, costs $2,344,000.

▷ Golf bags were initiated around 1895. Before then, players or caddies carried clubs and equipment by hand.

▷ Every hole at the Manila Golf and Country Club was named after a different species of tree on the course: Narra, Acacia, Chico, Dao, Pili, Caballero, Santol, Banana, Avocado, Guava, Launa, Kakawate, Nanka, Ipil, Tamarind, Agoho, Dapdap, and Mango.

▷ The first hole-in-one ever recorded was by Tom Morris, Jr., in the 1868 Open Championship, on the eighth hole at Prestwick.

▷ Schlaff—meaning that the ball has been mis-hit because the clubhead has hit the ground first—is one of the oldest terms in golf and is probably of ancient Scottish origin. In the States we say that the shot was hit "fat." Maybe "schlaff" is more appropriate, just because of the sound of the word!

▷ Longest hole-in-one on a straightway by a man: 447 yards by Robert Mitera, of Omaha, Nebraska, on the 10th hole at the Miracle Hills Golf Club, Omaha, Nebraska.

▷ Longest hole-in-one on a straightway by a woman: 393 yards by Marie Robie, Wollaston, Massachusetts, on the first hole at Furnace Brook Golf Club, Wollaston, Massachusetts, in 1949.

▷ Most holes-in-one during a single round: three by Dr. Joseph Boydstone, Bakersfield, California, on the third, fourth, and ninth holes at the Bakersfield Country Club on October 10, 1962.

▷ Longest double eagle by a man: 647 yards, by Chief

Petty Officer Kevin Murray on the second hole at the Guam Navy Golf Club in 1982.

▷ Longest double eagle by a woman: 509 yards, by Mrs. William Jenkins, Sr., of Baltimore, Maryland, on the 12th hole at Longview Golf Club in Cockeysville, Maryland, 1965.

▷ Electric golf carts were first used for golf at the Thunderbird Golf Club, United States, 1949.

▷ Golf clubhead covers were first sold at St. Andrews, Scotland, in 1916. They were designed by a Japanese student, Seilchi Takahata, while in England.

▷ "The yips" is a term that was first coined by professional Tommy Armour in the 1930s to describe the nervous twitch that afflicts many golfers when putting.

▷ The most consecutive birdies in one round was 10, achieved by professional John Irwin at the St. Catharine's Golf and Country Club, Ontario, Canada, in 1984.

▷ The world's longest course is the par-77, 8,325-yard International Golf Club, Bolton, Massachusetts.

▷ Longest par 3: 270 yards, 16th, International Golf Club, Bolton, Massachusetts.

▷ Longest par 4: 500 yards, sixth, Eisenhower Golf Club, City of Industry, California.

▷ Longest par 5: 710 yards, 17th, Palmira Golf and Country Club, St. Johns, Indiana.

▷ Longest par 6: 747 yards, 17th, Black Mountain Golf Course, North Carolina.

▷ Longest par 7: 948 yards, sixth, Koolan Island Golf Club, Western Australia.

▷ Largest Tournament: the Volkswagen Grand Prix Open Amateur Championship (U.K.), which attracted a record 321,778 competitors (206,820 men, and 114,958 women) in 1984.

▷ Francis Brown, a golf addict, was tried in the courts at Banff, Scotland, for stealing two golf balls, found guilty, and hanged in 1637.

▷ Fewest putts by a man for 18 holes was 15, by professional Richard Stanwood of Caldwell, Idaho, in 1976, and by amateur Ed Drysdale of Cheraw, Colorado, in 1985.

▷ Fewest putts by a woman for 18 holes was 17, by professional Joan Joyce of Stratford, Connecticut, in 1982 and 19 by amateur Beverly Whitaker of Pasadena, California.

▷ Fastest round of golf: 77 players completed the 18-hole, 6,502-yard Kern City, California, course in 10 minutes, 30 seconds on August 24, 1984, using only one ball and scoring an 80!

▷ There are approximately 85 golf club manufacturers in the United States.

▷ The most aces shot in one year is 33 by Scott Palmer, a feat accomplished from June 5, 1983, to May 31, 1984, all on holes between 130 and 350 yards in length in San Diego County, California.

▷ The greatest number of holes-in-one reported in a career is 97, by Scott Palmer of San Diego, California, who was born in 1958.

▷ The largest green in the world is reputed to be the par-6, 695-yard fifth hole at International Golf Club, Bolton, Massachusetts, with an area greater than 28,000 square feet. That translates into a square with 167-foot sides.

▷ The lowest score for 18 holes was scored by English professional Alfred Edward Smith, who shot a 55 on his home course in 1936.

▷ The first postage stamp in the world related to golf was issued by Japan in 1953. The United States and the United Kingdom didn't issue one until 1973.

▷ International team matches started with amateurs, England versus Scotland, in 1902. England won 32 holes while Scotland won 25 holes.

▷ India was the first country outside of Great Britain to play golf, and that was in 1829.

▷ The lowest score with one club was a recorded score of 70 (two under par) on the 6,037-yard Lochmere Golf Club course in Cary, North Carolina, and shot with a driver by Thad Daber of Durham, North Carolina, in 1987.

▷ The longest officially recorded long drive was accomplished by Jack Hamm of Denver when he drove the ball 406 yards in 1986. This was done in an official PGA long driving contest in which the drive had to land in a fairway only 40 feet wide.

▷ Byron Nelson holds the record for winning the most tournaments in a single season. He won 18, 11 of them consecutively, also a record, in 1945.

▷ Longest putt: Bob Cook (United States) sank a putt measured at 140 feet 2¾ inches on the 18th at St. Andrews, Scotland, in a professional-amateur tournament on October 1, 1976.

▷ The highest golf course in the world is the Tuctu Golf Club in Morococha, Peru, which is 14,335 feet above sea level at its lowest point.

▷ The lowest golf course in the world is Furnace Creek Golf Course, Death Valley, California, which is approximately 178 feet below sea level.

▷ Golf is a $20-billion-a-year industry worldwide, while in the United States it is a $5.2 billion industry. In 1988, golf equipment had total sales of $3.1 billion.

▷ Golf is the game of choice for 80 percent of the CEOs of major corporations, according to a survey taken in 1988.

▷ In 1989 purse money on the PGA Tour was approximately $42 million.

▷ There are approximately 23.4 million golfers in the United States.

▷ An estimated 487 million rounds of golf were played in the United States in 1989.

▷ In the United States there are approximately 13,626 golf courses, of which 8,300 or so are private or semi-private.

▷ Japan has an estimated 11,300,000 golfers and only 1,558 golf courses. You think *your* golf course is crowded!

▷ The census of world golf indicates that there are close to 50 million golfers in the world who play on a total of 24,000 golf facilities.

▷ According to 1984 and 1988 figures, golf is played in 76 countries of the world. In Russia there are apparently no golf courses.

▷ The five countries with the most golfers, along with the golf facilities available in those countries, are as follows:

United States	23,400,000	13,626
Japan	11,300,000	1,558
Canada	2,200,000	1,796
England	596,000	1,300
Korea	500,000	43

▷ The oldest golf club in the world is reported to be the "Honourable Company of Edinburgh Golfers," which came into existence in 1744.

▷ The state of Florida has more golf courses than any other state in the country, with 1,000 operating and 45 under construction. The 1,000 courses, if laid out in a straight line, would be approximately 3,500 miles long.

▷ Which of the following golf balls have you played with during your years of playing the game? Be careful, the golf balls you say you have used could possibly date you!

feathery	Red Dot	Rocket
gutty	Maxfli	Slazenger
gutta-percha	Colonel	Status
Acme	Star Challenger	Eagle
Ocobo	Why Not	Titleist—Balata
Silvertown	Triumph	Excalibur ELT
Glory Dimple	Clackheaton	416
Green Circle	Colonel Click	Top-Flite Plus
Black Circle	Bullet Honor	Hogan
Spalding Dot	Kro-Flite	Pinnacle
Baby Dimple	Silver King	Wilson Pro Staff
Haskell Whiz	Vardon Flyer	Ultra
Red Honor	Hot Dog	Condor

Golden Ram	Ram Tour	Maxfli Tour LTD
Laser 392	Dunlop XLT-15	MD
Bullet	MacGregor	Pinnacle Gold
Dunlop Red	Master	Maxfli Master
Circle	Flying Lady	Top-Flite XL
Molitor	Spalding Elite	Maxfli DDH III
Bridgestone	Golden Ram	Top-Flite II
Precept	Ping	
Tour Edition	Titleist DT	

▷ The following names are the ancient precursors of the modern set of golf clubs. How many clubs do you have in your golf bag? Imagine playing a round of golf with just the following:

Brassie—the term for what today would be a two-wood

Spoon—term for what today would be a three-wood

Cleek—term for what today would be a two- or three-iron

Mashie—ancient lofted club equivalent to a five-iron today

Mashie Niblick—ancient lofted club equivalent to a seven-iron

Niblick—ancient lofted club equivalent to a nine-iron

▷ The oldest recorded playing foursome had a cumulative age of 361 and consisted of Maurice Pease, 98, Joseph Hooker, 94, Richerdson Bronson, 85, and Stanley Hart, Sr., the youngster at 84.

▷ Most consecutive one-putt greens: 18, by Rick Coverdale of Baltimore, Maryland, in 1958, and by Johnny

Pallot of Coral Gables, Florida, in 1981.

▷ Fastest round of golf on foot was 28 minutes, 9 seconds, accomplished by Gary Wright on the 6,039-yard Tewantin-Noosa Golf Club, Queensland, Australia, in 1980.

▷ Most recorded golf courses played in a lifetime is 3,625 by Ralph Kennedy of New York, New York.

▷ The bouncing ball record is held by Mark Mooney of Hummelstown, Pennsylvania, who bounced a ball off the face of his pitching wedge 1,764 times.

▷ Annual golf ball sales around the world total approximately 500 million dollars or over 20 million dozen golf balls!

▷ Women make up 23 percent of the total golfing population; however, 41 percent of new golfers are women.

THE SIDE GAMES WE PLAY & WAGER: GROUP THREE

The games in this chapter for the most part include a higher level of betting or wagering than the previously described games. In some cases the games allow for a change of partners on every hole or a new bet on every hole. Some of the games allow a player or team to decide their own fate by having a player pick a partner or by having a team bid on what their total score will be for a hole.

In some of the following games, strategy is definitely a factor not only in how one plays a hole but in how one bets that hole. You will also find some interesting formats for both threesome and fivesome play. With all the bets, and the potential press bets, coupled with any Garbarge games that might be played, an accountant in the group would prove beneficial in determining who wins and who loses money at the end of the round!

Remember: you are out to have fun, so if you can't lose it, don't bet it!

CENTER OR RIGHT
ONE-HALF AGGREGATE SCORE
FOUR-BALL FOURSOME
LOW BALLS OF FOURSOME
FIVESOME WHEEL
BEST BALL FOURSOME
AVERAGE SCORE
EVERY THREE HOLES
ECLECTIC
AUTOMATICS
EIGHTY-ONE or NINES
TWELVES

SIXTEENS

LAS VEGAS

DAYTONA

LAS VEGAS, AZ

HAWK, WOLF, or CAPTAIN

THREESOME HAWK

HOG

WOLF AND PIG FIVESOME

THE DOG

BRIDGE

BACKGAMMON or DOUBLE

SIX, SIX, AND SIX, or RANSOME

REJECT or WIPE-OUT

CENTER OR RIGHT

After deciding the teeing-off order for the foursome, everyone tees off and teams are decided by the two drives that are closest to the center or the two drives that are farthest to the right. The two teams then play for 2 points a hole: 1 point for low score and 1 point for low-total score. If there is a tie on the hole, then the teams stay the same for the next hole. If there is no tie, then the player designated as the second player on the first hole tees off first on the second hole, and so on, until the fifth hole. There, providing there have been no ties, the player who teed off first on the first hole tees off first again. At the end of the round, everyone's points are totaled and the difference between player points determines who pays whom, and how much.

ONE-HALF AGGREGATE SCORE

This is a game played when there are only three players and the players are of reasonably equal playing ability. The game is broken up into six-hole matches with one player for the first six holes playing against one-half of the aggregate score of the two other players. For example, if Player A and Player B are teamed for the first six holes and score a 4 and a 5 on the first hole, then Player C has to beat $4\frac{1}{2}$ on the first hole in order to win. The same format is used for the next five holes.

The second six-hole match starts on the seventh hole, with Player A playing against one-half the aggregate score of Player B and Player C on holes 7 through 12. The third match would therefore cover holes 13 through 18 using the same format. You can play each match for a set amount or you can play that each point won is worth a set amount. At the end of the 18 holes, add everyone's pluses and minuses and the player or players with the minuses pay the player or players with the pluses.

FOUR-BALL FOURSOME

This is played with two players on a side with each playing his or her own ball. The low ball of each team counts on each hole, with the low ball of the foursome winning that hole. The team that has the most low balls on the most holes wins the match. This is also fun to play when you have two or more foursomes out playing and you play the same format but with the low ball of the foursome counting toward the match with the other foursomes. We play this with each player putting a set wager into the pot. Then the foursome that has the most low balls on the most holes wins the pot and divides it among the four players. (See score-card example 3-1.)

"The hardest shot is a mashie [five-iron] at 90 yards from the green, where the ball has to be played against an oak tree, bounces back into a sand trap, hits a stone, bounces on the green, and then rolls into the cup. That shot is so difficult that I have only made it once."

—Zeppo Marx

FOURBALL FOURSOME

Scorecard 3-1

HOLE	1	2	3	4	5	6	7	8	9	Out
Black Tees	422	347	107	598	392	239	454	517	414	3490
Gold Tees	386	336	104	512	361	230	416	474	364	3183
Silver Tees	353	272	67	486	329	188	370	447	350	2862
PAR	4	4	3	5	4	3	4	5	4	36
Handicap	7	15	17	3	11	9	1	5	13	
PLAYER A (25)	5	6	4	7	5	4	(6)	5	7	49
B (23)	6	5	4	6	6	5	6	6	6	50
BEST BALL WIN				1						
PLAYER C (24)	5	5	3	8	5	5	(6)	5	6	48
D (25)	4	5	4	7	6	4	(5)	7	5	47
BEST BALL WIN	1		1				1		1	

Here Players A and B play against Players C and D. In this example, players play off Player B's handicap (handicaps are in parentheses), so Player A gets two shots, Player C one shot, and Player D two shots. Handicap holes are circled.

INITIALS	10	11	12	13	14	15	16	17	18	In	Tot	Hcp	Net
	362	445	548	324	183	435	169	403	589	3458	6948		
	337	406	509	281	150	413	139	374	564	3173	6356		
	326	377	443	255	95	335	116	349	503	2799	5661		
	4	4	5	4	3	4	3	4	5	36	72		
	16	6	4	12	14	2	18	8	10				
A	5	6	6	4	4	⑥	4	6	7	48	97		
B	4	5	7	5	3	5	5	6	6	46	96		
	1			1							3		
C	6	5	7	4	4	6	4	6	6	48	96		
D	5	7	6	5	4	⑥	4	5	6	48	95		
							1				5		

As indicated here, Players C and D win five best ball holes while Players A and B win three best ball holes. As a result, Players C and D win 2 points each from their opponents.

LOW BALLS OF FOURSOME

There are no predetermined partners in this game; however, partners are decided by the two players who shoot the two lowest scores on each individual hole. The points that are lost or won are determined by the difference in the total score between the two low balls and the two high balls. For instance, if two players each score a 4 while the other two players score a 5 and a 6, the point differential is 3 (8 versus 11). The point value is decided before the start of play. If there is a three-way tie for low ball or if there is a tie for second low ball, no points are earned or lost for that hole.

FIVESOME WHEEL

This fivesome game involves a preselected twosome playing a match against the other three players that form three twosomes. For example, if by ball toss Players D and E are the two closest balls, they become the wheel team and play against Players A, B, and C. These three players form three twosomes, AB, AC, and BC, who each play a separate match against the wheel team of DE. Usually full handicaps are used in this game. However, some play off the low-handicap player and have their handicaps adjusted accordingly, with the low-handicap player thus playing as a zero. The games that can be played among the four teams vary tremendously; however, the games played most often are: a net best ball low score for the 18 holes, a high-low point game, and regular Nassau with presses when a team is 2 down. If your team is the wheel, it's to be hoped that you are on your game, for otherwise it could be an expensive day.

BEST BALL FOURSOME

This game is somewhat similar to the previously described four-ball foursome except that at least two foursomes are required, one foursome playing against the other. The twist to this game is that the score of each member of the foursome contributes to the team score on a minimum of 3 of the 18 holes. Whether playing against another foursome or three or four foursomes, each team scores their best ball (or balls) as follows: on the first hole, the best ball of the foursome is recorded; then, on the second hole, the two best balls of the foursome are recorded for a team total; then, on the third hole, the three best balls are recorded as a team total; then, on the fourth hole, the team's total score for all four players is recorded as a team total. After the fourth hole, the scoring process is again repeated, starting on the fifth hole, the ninth hole, and the 13th hole. On the 17th hole, only the best ball of the foursome is used for the team score; while on the 18th hole, the two best balls of the foursome are used for the team score.

The team that has the lowest total score for the 18 holes is the winner. In the case of one foursome playing against another, each player on the winning team wins the predetermined bet. When more than two foursomes are playing, you can then have an individual bet with the other foursomes or you can agree to every player putting $1 or $5 into the pot, with the winning foursome splitting the pot among themselves.

This game can also be played so that everyone gets his or her full handicap and takes the handicap strokes where they fall on the scorecard. Providing that pros, amateur pros, or all low handicappers are not playing, a team score in the range of 180–190 is good, especially if you're using gross scores.

AVERAGE SCORE

This game is played with partners playing against the rest of the field using their individual gross scores as a means of determining their team score. Each partner plays each hole and then averages the total score to determine the team score. After completing their rounds, they subtract one-half of their combined handicap from their 18-hole total to determine their net score. Half strokes count as whole strokes after totaling. You might wager against other teams based upon the difference in the team net scores, or you might even arrange Nassau bets based on your average scores.

> *"Bob, you can't always be playing well when it counts. You'll never win golf tournaments until you learn to score well when you're playing badly."*
>
> —Jim Barnes, teaching professional, giving advice to a young Bobby Jones

EVERY THREE HOLES

This is a good game for five players. It is like a Nassau, but you change partners every three holes so that one player always has two other players as individual partners. In essence, there are three two-player teams, each playing against the other. When I've played this game, we play that either best ball or low-total score wins the hole. Another variation I've played has automatic presses when you go 1 down. A team might go 1 up on the first hole and then lose the second hole and thereby be even on the first bet and down on the second bet. Then, if they lose the third hole they will end up 1 down on the original bet, 2 down on the second bet, and 1 down on the third bet because of the second automatic press that took effect after the second hole.

After three holes you throw balls in the air to decide who will be partners for the next three holes. The player who did not have two individual partners now becomes the swing player. After every player has had the chance to be the swing player, allow the player who is losing the most the option to be the swing player for the last three holes. Add up everyone's pluses and minuses to decide who pays whom. At times we have found that all the matches and the automatic presses, and the fact that we also play Skins, Sandies, and Proxies, result in an accounting nightmare that requires all five players to push a pencil to determine who has won and who has lost.

> *"Golferswhotalkfastswingfast."*
> —Bob Toski, *Golf Digest*, 1982

ECLECTIC

This game can be played either individually or with two-player teams. The game itself can be played in two different manners. The first method involves the selection of nine holes drawn out of a hat or cup after everyone has completed play, with the nine holes consisting of two par 3s, two par 5s, and five par 4s. The winner is the player with the lowest best ball score or total team score for those nine holes.

The other method of playing this game uses the best or lowest score achieved by a player or a team on two of the par 3s, two of the par 5s, and five of the par 4s out of the 18 holes played.

With either method, usually one-half of a player's handicap is used.

AUTOMATICS

I have heard of this being played only by golfers with low handicaps. Basically, Automatics is a game in which a new bet starts on every hole regardless of the results on the previous hole. Even if you tie the first hole it still means that going off the second tee you are even and 0, depending on how you do on that hole. If perchance you win the second hole, that means you go to the third tee + 1, + 1, and 0. After nine holes in a game like this, the players should have a minimum of eight matches besides any other bets, wagers, or Garbarge being played. In a game like Automatics you need a lot of scorecard and a lot of lead in the pencil.

The game becomes even more complex from a scoring standpoint if you play both individual as well as team Automatics. In this event I strongly encourage engaging the services of a certified public accountant who can keep the columns of bets straight (with the debits and credits going into the proper player columns), and can provide a reasonable accounting of who won and who lost at the end of the match!

EIGHTY-ONE or NINES

When you are short a player and have only a threesome, this is a good game. Each hole has a total point value of 9, and 9 times 9 holes is 81—thus the name of the game. Players either play heads up (with no handicap) or with full handicap, taking shots where they fall on the scorecard. The winner of the hole, the player with the best score, is awarded 5 points; the player with the next-best score gets 3 points; and the player with the high score gets 1 point. In the case of two players tying for best score, split the first and second points so that they each get 4 points. If all three players tie for the low score, then each player gets 3 points. When two players tie for the high score, split the second and third points so that each gets 2 points.

Prior to playing, decide how much each point is worth. The point value can be anything that you and the others decide. The total points at the end of nine holes should be 81, and the same for the back nine, so that the total of all players' points at the end of 18 holes should be 162. Totaling the points for all players determines who pays whom, with the low-point-total player paying both the other players based on the

EIGHTY-ONE or NINES

Scorecard 3-2

HOLE	1	2	3	4	5	6	7	8	9	Out
Black Tees	422	347	107	598	392	239	454	517	414	3490
Gold Tees	386	336	104	512	361	230	416	474	364	3183
Silver Tees	353	272	67	486	329	188	370	447	350	2862
PAR	4	4	3	5	4	3	4	5	4	36
Handicap	7	15	17	3	11	9	1	5	13	
PLAYER A (12)	⑤	4	3	⑥	⑤	③	④	⑤	4	39
PTS.	2	4	3	2	3	4	5	3	4	30
B (14)	⑤	5	3	⑤	⑥	⑤	⑤	⑤	⑤	44
PTS.	2	1	3	5	1	1	2	3	4	22
C (11)	④	4	3	⑥	④	③	⑤	⑤	5	39
PTS.	5	4	3	2	5	4	2	3	1	29

Players A, B, and C get full handicaps, with handicap holes circled, and the points won on each hole are indicated below each player's score.

INITIALS	10	11	12	13	14	15	16	17	18	In	Tot	Hcp	Net
	362	445	548	324	183	435	169	403	589	3458	6948		
	337	406	509	281	150	413	139	374	564	3173	6356		
	326	377	443	255	95	335	116	349	503	2799	5661		
	4	4	5	4	3	4	3	4	5	36	72		
	16	6	4	12	14	2	18	8	10				
A	5	(5)	(7)	(3)	3	(4)	4	(6)	(6)	43	82		
	2	2	1	5	2	4	3	1	3	23	53		
B	5	(4)	(5)	(6)	(3)	(5)	4	(4)	(6)	42	86		
	2	5	5	2	5	1	3	3	3	29	51		
C	4	(5)	(6)	5	3	(4)	4	(3)	(6)	40	79		
	5	2	3	2	2	4	3	5	3	29	58		

In this example, Player C wins 58 total points and would win 7 points from Player B, who had 51 total points, and win 5 points from Player A, who had 53 total points. Note that all player points add up to 81 on the front side and 81 on the back side to total 162 points.

point differential. The player with the second highest
point total also pays the high-point player based on
the point differential. (See scorecard example 3-2.)

TWELVES

This is a game similar to Eighty-One, but it is played
by a foursome, with each individual playing against
the others in the foursome. It can be played by low
handicappers as a gross score game or by mixed-level
handicappers as a net score game. In Twelves, points
are won on each hole based upon performance, with
the point breakdown on each hole as follows: the low
score wins 6 points, the second-low score wins 4
points, the third-low score wins 2 points, and the high
score on the hole gets no points. In the case of a two-
way tie for low score, the players split the points for
low and second-low score so that they each win 5
points. In the case of a three-way tie for low score,
each player wins 4 points, and in the case of a four-
way tie each player wins 3 points. Ties for second-low
score or for high score would be handled in a similar
fashion, with the available points being split equally
among the players. The total of all player points on
each of the nine holes should be 108.

Some players like to play this game because they do
not have to depend upon a partner and can concen-
trate on their own game. However, some also play this
game in conjunction with some of the Garbarge games
or a Nassau.

The winner in Twelves is the player with the most
points at the end of the round. This player is paid by
the other players an amount equal to the difference in

their point totals times whatever each point is worth.

As an example, you are playing for 10 cents and Player A has 59 points, Player B has 54 points, Player C has 64 points, and Player D has 39 points. Therefore Players A, B, and D all pay Player C as follows:

A: 64 points (Player C) − 59 points (Player A) = 5 points;

$$5 \times 10 \text{ cents} = 50 \text{ cents}$$

B: 64 points (Player C) − 54 points (Player B) = 10 points;

$$10 \times 10 \text{ cents} = \$1$$

D: 64 points (Player C) − 39 points (Player D) = 25 points;

$$25 \times 10 \text{ cents} = \$2.50$$

Points for the entire game should total 216. (See scorecard example 3-3.)

> *"The job of a finishing hole is as clearly defined as that of a dance hall bouncer. It has to maintain order, clear out the amateurs, and preserve the dignity of the game."*
> —Jim Murray, *Golf* magazine, 1983

TWELVES

Scorecard 3-3

HOLE	1	2	3	4	5	6	7	8	9	Out
Black Tees	422	347	107	598	392	239	454	517	414	3490
Gold Tees	386	336	104	512	361	230	416	474	364	3183
Silver Tees	353	272	67	486	329	188	370	447	350	2862
PAR	4	4	3	5	4	3	4	5	4	36
Handicap	7	15	17	3	11	9	1	5	13	
PLAYER A (12)	⑤	4	3	⑥	⑤	③	④	⑤	4	39
	3	4	4	3	4	5	6	4	3	36
B (14)	⑤	5	3	⑤	⑥	⑤	⑤	⑤	⑤	44
	3	0	4	6	1	0	2	4	3	23
C (11)	④	4	3	⑥	④	③	⑤	⑤	5	39
	6	4	4	3	6	5	2	4	0	34
D (15)	⑥	⑤	4	⑦	⑥	④	⑤	⑥	④	47
	0	4	0	0	1	2	2	0	6	15

This game is similar to Eighty-One or Nines but is played by a foursome with points earned as follows: low score 6 points, second-low score 4 points, third-low score 2 points. The high scorer earns no points. In this example, players play with full handicaps, with handicap holes being circled. Points won, if any, are below the player's score.

INITIALS	10	11	12	13	14	15	16	17	18	In	Tot	Hcp	Net
	362	445	548	324	183	435	169	403	589	3458	6948		
	337	406	509	281	150	413	139	374	564	3173	6356		
	326	377	443	255	95	335	116	349	503	2799	5661		
	4	4	5	4	3	4	3	4	5	36	72		
	16	6	4	12	14	2	18	8	10				
A	5	(5)	(7)	(3)	3	(4)	4	(6)	(6)	43	82		
	2	2	0	6	1	5	4	1	2	23	59	TOTAL PTS.	
B	5	(4)	(5)	(6)	(3)	(5)	4	(4)	(6)	42	86		
	2	6	6	1	5	1	4	4	2	31	54	TOTAL PTS.	
C	4	(5)	(6)	5	3	(4)	4	(3)	(6)	40	79		
	6	2	3	1	1	5	4	6	2	30	64	TOTAL PTS.	
D	5	(5)	(6)	(5)	(3)	(5)	5	(6)	(5)	45	92		
	2	2	3	4	5	1	0	1	6	24	39	TOTAL PTS.	

As indicated here, Player C wins with a high point total of 64 points and therefore wins from Player A 5 points (64−59), from Player B 10 points (64−54), and from Player D 25 points (64−39).

SIXTEENS

In this foursome game, each individual plays against the others in a fashion similar to that in Twelves. As in Twelves, this game can be played by both low and high handicappers as a gross or net score game. In Sixteens points are won on each hole based upon the following performance: low score wins 7 points, second-low score wins 5 points, third-low score wins 3 points, and the high score on the hole wins 1 point.

Ties are handled in a similar fashion to that in Twelves, with the points equally split among the players who tie. For example, if three players tie for low score, then each player wins 5 points and the high score wins 1 point; or if two players tie for low score and two players tie for high score, the low-score players each win 6 points while the high-score players each win 2 points.

As in Twelves, this game can be played in conjunction with some of the Garbarge games or even a Nassau match. The winner in Sixteens is the player at the end of the round with the highest point total. The winner is then paid by the other players based on point differentials times the value of each point. The same method is used to pay both second- and third-high-point players. In Sixteens the total of all player points should equal 144 for each nine holes, or 288 points for the 18-hole round. As a check, remember that on each hole the total of all the players' points won should equal 16.

LAS VEGAS

This game is usually played by one twosome against another twosome, and the individual scores of each twosome are compared. In comparing scores, the low ball followed by the other score determines the points won or lost. A twosome that scores two 4s is said to have a 44 (4-4) and if their opponents get a 4 and a 5 the opponents have a 45 (4-5), and the original twosome wins 1 point (45 − 44 = 1). If the score of a twosome is 44 (4-4) versus a 56 (5-6), then the low twosome wins 12 points.

This game gets dangerous because if the winning twosome wins by scoring a birdie, then the points being played for are *doubled* on that hole. For instance, if one team scores a birdie 3 and a par 4 (3-4) and the other team a par 4 and a bogey 5 (4-5), then the twosome having the birdie wins a total of 22 points (45 − 34 = 11 × 2 = 22). While birdies result in a doubling of the points, an eagle results in a *tripling* of the points. Thus this can definitely be a game in which the lead changes an amazing number of times. (See scorecard example 3-4.)

> *"You can be the greatest iron player in the world, or the greatest putter, but if you can't get the ball in position to use your greatness, you can't win."*
> —Ben Hogan, on the importance of drives

LAS VEGAS

Scorecard 3-4

HOLE	1	2	3	4	5	6	7	8	9	Out
Black Tees	422	347	107	598	392	239	454	517	414	3490
Gold Tees	386	336	104	512	361	230	416	474	364	3183
Silver Tees	353	272	67	486	329	188	370	447	350	2862
PAR	4	4	3	5	4	3	4	5	4	36
Handicap	7	15	17	3	11	9	1	5	13	
PLAYER A (12)	5	4	3	6	5	3	4	5	4	
B (14)	5	5	3	5	6	5	5	5	5	
	55	45	33	56	56	35	45	55	45	
PLAYER C (11)	4	4	3	6	4	3	5	5	5	
D (15)	6	5	4	7	6	4	5	6	4	
	46	45	34	67	46	34	55	56	45	
TEAM PTS. WON/LOST	-9	-	+1	+11	-10	-1	+10	+1	-	+3
CUMULATIVE TOTAL	-9	-9	-8	+3	-7	-8	+2	+3	+3	+3

Here Team AB plays against Team CD and the teams are playing even. The scoring is from Team AB's standpoint in regard to team points won or lost.

INITIALS	10	11	12	13	14	15	16	17	18	In	Tot	Hcp	Net
	362	445	548	324	183	435	169	403	589	3458	6948		
	337	406	509	281	150	413	139	374	564	3173	6356		
	326	377	443	255	95	335	116	349	503	2799	5661		
	4	4	5	4	3	4	3	4	5	36	72		
	16	6	4	12	14	2	18	8	10				
A	5	5	7	3	3	4	4	6	6				
B	5	4	5	6	3	5	4	4	6				
	55	45	57	36	33	45	44	46	66				
C	4	5	6	5	3	4	4	3	6				
D	5	5	6	5	3	5	5	6	5				
	45	55	66	55	33	45	45	36	56				
	-10	+10	+9	+38	-	-	+1	-20	-10	+18			
	-10	-	+9	+47	+47	+47	+48	+28	+18	+18	+21		

Team AB in this example wins the front side +3 and wins the back side +18, mainly due to the birdie by Player A on hole 13, which doubled their point winnings on that hole. Team AB wins from Team CD a total of 21 points for the 18 holes.

DAYTONA

This game, a stroke-play partner game best suited for low handicappers, is somewhat similar to Las Vegas. Taking a par 4, if both partners score 4s their score is 44; however, if one of the partners scores a birdie (or better) that score comes first to produce a team score of 34. If one of the partners scores a bogey or worse, then that score comes first in the partnership score. So if a partner has a double-bogey 6, the team score would be 64. At the end of play the partnership with the higher point total pays out the agreed unit value times the point difference in the two team totals. Clearly, the scoring can fluctuate wildly. Those double bogeys and triple bogeys can really hurt!

LAS VEGAS, AZ

This is another game in which one twosome plays against another. In this format of Las Vegas, the scores of each twosome are multiplied and then compared. The difference determines what the high scorers pay to the low scorers. As an example, say that one twosome scores a 4 and a 5, so that their score is 20 (4 × 5), while their opponents score a 5 and a 5, so that their score is 25 (5 × 5). The differential in this case is five (25 − 20) and the twosome that scored the 25 loses 5 points, while the twosome that scored the 20 wins 5 points. As another example, let's say that one twosome scores 4s for a total of 16, while their opponents score a 4 and a 7 for a total of 28. The members of the team that had the 28 lose 12 points

(28 − 16) each, and the members of the team that had the 16 win 12 points each.

One of the players who plays Las Vegas, AZ is in the insurance business and plays with a "stop loss," which limits the high score on any hole for any player to a maximum of a triple bogey. In this game, as in others, you decide beforehand the value of each point. Also, points lost or won apply to each player of the twosome. Some golfers play that in the case of a twosome that wins the low score total with a birdie, the points won are doubled on that hole. To determine who wins and who loses, add up all the pluses and minuses, and the twosome with plus points wins their points times the predetermined value of each point. (See scorecard example 3-5.)

HAWK, WOLF, or CAPTAIN

This is played with a foursome. The first player to tee off becomes the hawk (or the wolf or the captain). Each player becomes the hawk on subsequent holes until the fifth hole, when the player who was the hawk on the first hole again becomes the hawk. After everyone has teed off, the hawk picks his or her partner from among the other three players. Naturally, the hawk picks the player with the safest and best drive. The hawk and the partner must then beat their opponents by best ball. If they don't, they lose; or, if there is a tie, there is no blood and neither team wins. The hawk, however, can decide to play a hole without a partner and play against the other three players. In this case, the hawk must beat the best ball of the other

LAS VEGAS, AZ

Scorecard 3-5

HOLE	1	2	3	4	5	6	7	8	9	Out
Black Tees	422	347	107	598	392	239	454	517	414	3490
Gold Tees	386	336	104	512	361	230	416	474	364	3183
Silver Tees	353	272	67	486	329	188	370	447	350	2862
PAR	4	4	3	5	4	3	4	5	4	36
Handicap	7	15	17	3	11	9	1	5	13	
PLAYER A (12)	5	4	3	6	5	3	4	5	4	
PLAYER B (14)	5	5	3	5	6	5	5	5	5	
	25	20	9	30	30	15	20	25	20	
PLAYER C (11)	4	4	3	6	4	3	5	5	5	
PLAYER D (15)	6	5	4	7	6	4	5	6	4	
	24	20	12	42	24	12	25	30	20	
TEAM POINTS										
WON/LOST	-1	-	+3	+12	-6	-3	+5	+5	-	+15

In this game Team AB is playing against Team CD with teams playing even. The scoring is from Team AB's standpoint in regard to points won or lost. Remember, in this game twosome scores are multiplied to result in a total score versus that of the other twosome.

INITIALS	10	11	12	13	14	15	16	17	18	In	Tot	Hcp	Net
	362	445	548	324	183	435	169	403	589	3458	6948		
	337	406	509	281	150	413	139	374	564	3173	6356		
	326	377	443	255	95	335	116	349	503	2799	5661		
	4	4	5	4	3	4	3	4	5	36	72		
	16	6	4	12	14	2	18	8	10				
A	5	5	7	3	3	4	4	6	6				
B	5	4	5	6	3	5	4	4	6				
	25	20	35	18	9	20	16	24	36				
C	4	5	6	5	3	4	4	3	6				
D	5	5	6	5	3	5	5	6	5				
	20	25	36	25	9	20	20	18	30				
	-5	+5	+1	+14	-	-	+4	-12	-6	+1	+16		

In this example, Team AB wins a total of 16 points from Team CD, 15 points on the front and 1 point on the back. Once again the birdie on hole 13 was a deciding factor in who won and who lost.

three players. When the hawk goes it alone then all bets are doubled, and if the hawk loses he or she pays each of the other three players double the bet.

Hawk can be played using full handicaps, which can result in some decision making by the hawk, especially when deciding to take a partner who gets a shot. Since two holes are left after every player has been the hawk four times, the player who has lost the most bets gets to be the hawk for holes 17 and 18. As I have found out many times, the two best drives of a hole do not necessarily guarantee that the hawk team will have the best ball. I have seen some amazing birdies made out of the rough to win the best ball. There was also the case of a player hitting a shot out of bounds off the tee but nevertheless shooting a bogey 5 to win the best ball. The bet value in this game is determined before the start of play and remains the same for each hole.

THREESOME HAWK

With only three players Hawk can still be played by having the missing fourth player become a bogey score for every hole played. The format is the same as that of a four-player game: you decide upon an order of play, and then after all players have hit their drives, the first player, who is the hawk, selects a partner prior to leaving the tee box. In Threesome Hawk, the hawk has a choice between the other two players or a bogey score for the hole as a partner. Low net score wins the hole. In the case of a tie, neither team wins nor loses and the second player becomes the hawk on the next tee box. This game also allows a player to go it alone on a par 3 or possibly on a tough par 4 or 5, especially when the other two players have driven into trouble off the tee. Remember that when a player does decide to go it alone, the bets or point values are doubled for that particular hole.

HOG

This game is just like the Hawk, Wolf, or Captain game—with one major exception: with the Hog format, the hog must select a player as a partner or not immediately after that player's tee shot; there is no waiting to see how the other players hit their tee shots and then selecting the best. Once a player has been rejected, that player cannot become the hog's partner regardless of what happens to the other players. If the hog fails to select Player C and then Player D hits a tee shot that's in trouble or out of bounds, the hog either selects Player D or decides to go it alone against the other three players. As in Hawk, a best ball format decides who wins each hole. If the hog goes it alone, the bet value is doubled. The bet can also be doubled by the opposing team after all players have hit their tee shots.

> *"It's a compromise of what your ego wants you to do, what experience tells you to do, and what your nerves let you do."*
> —Bruce Crampton, on tournament golf

WOLF AND PIG FIVESOME

In Wolf and Pig Fivesome, five players decide upon a numerical order, 1 through 5, by throwing golf balls or by flipping a tee. After the order has been established, the player who has been designated Player 1 becomes the wolf and tees off first, with the other players following in numerical order. After everyone has teed off, Player 1 selects a partner from among the other four players prior to leaving the tee box. The hole is then played with Player 1 (the wolf) and the selected partner playing a net best ball against the other three players. On the second hole Player 2 becomes the wolf and tees off first, followed by Players 3, 4, 5, and 1. Once again the player who is the wolf selects a partner of choice after all players have teed off. The same format is used on the next three holes, with Player 1 again becoming the wolf on the sixth hole. Remember that this is a net best ball between the wolf and the wolf's partner, and that the partner is selected before leaving the tee box.

What about the pig? If the player who is the wolf has a good drive and the other players' drives are in trouble, or out of bounds, then the wolf can decide to play the hole without a partner and play against the other four players. In such an event, which often happens on par 3s, the bet is doubled and it is said that the wolf becomes the pig!

In this game, the wolf team either wins or loses $1\frac{1}{2}$ points and the other three players win or lose 1 point each. Point totals are tallied at the end of the round, and the total pluses should equal the total minuses.

THE DOG

This is a threesome game, using full handicaps, consisting of six parts with points awarded for each part. The six parts are: two hind legs, two front paws, one tail, and one head. Each point is worth $1. Parts and points are won or lost only when a player shoots a score without being tied or beaten. In this game, if two tie all tie.

As an example, if Player A shoots a par on the first hole without being tied or beaten, then that player earns a point and has one hind leg. If Player A also shoots a par on the second hole and wins that hole, then Player A now has 2 points and two hind legs. If on the third hole Player A is tied by Player C, then no points or parts are won or lost. If on the fourth hole Player B shoots a par, then Player B earns 1 point and now has one hind leg. Player A, however, with 2 points and two hind legs, loses one of the hind legs and goes into the fifth hole with 2 points and one hind leg. On the fifth hole Player C shoots a par and therefore earns a point and one hind leg. Players A and B both lose their hind legs. Going into the sixth hole Player A has 2 points but no parts, Player B has 1 point and no parts, and Player C has 1 point and one hind leg. If Player C comes into the 18th hole having five parts of the dog and 7 points and shoots a par on the 18th, and wins the hole, Player C is said to have won the dog. Player C, having won the dog and having earned 8 points, wins from each of the other players twice the point total. If Player C had been tied on the 18th and had a high point total of 7, then the other players would have each paid Player C $7. If two players tie in parts at the end of 18 holes, then the player with the most points wins.

In summary, parts and points are earned only when a player shoots a par or wins a hole without being tied. If two tie all tie, and no parts or points are won or lost. If another player shoots a par while others have a part or parts of the dog, those players each lose one part of the dog but do not lose their previously earned points. The player who ends the round with the most parts is the winner and is paid by each of the others the total earned points. If a player wins the dog (has all six parts), then the winning points are doubled. If a player wins the dog early in the round, start another game for the remaining holes.

BRIDGE

Bridge, which is played with partners, is a little more complex than some of the other games in that it requires both planning and strategy by the partners.

The game involves a team's bidding what they believe their aggregate score on a hole will be. The opposing team can accept this bid or can double the bet believing that the bid will not be achieved. The opposing team can also underbid the original bid, which means that they now have to achieve the aggregate score of their bid. In this situation the team that was underbid can also double the bet. Another variable is that the team that's been doubled can redouble the bet.

As an example, let's say that you and your partner start the action on the par-4 first hole and that you are playing for $1 a point. On the first tee, you and your partner both feel that you can par the hole so you bid an 8. The bid is accepted by the other team and you and your partner play the hole in an effort to score an aggregate 8 or better. If your team achieves a score of 8, you each win 1 point, or $1. If your team achieves a score of 7 you would each win 2 points, or $2.

If, however, you end up with an aggregate score over your bid, you and your partner lose a point for each shot that exceeds your bid. If, for example, still using the example bid of 8, you and your partner score a 4 and a 6 for a total of 10 (two shots over your bid), you each lose 2 points, or $2.

As another example, let's say the second hole is a tough par 5 and therefore your team bids an 11. The opposing team thinks about doubling you since they know that your partner never plays this hole well, but instead your opponents decide to take the bid away from you by bidding 10. Your team then doubles the bet, since you don't deem your opponents capable of achieving their bid. Your opponents, however, are confident they can, so they *redouble* the bet. In this situation each point is now worth $4.

In this example, if the bidding team shot a 4 and a 5 for an aggregate score of 9, versus its 10 bid, the team would win 2 points, with each player winning $8 since the original bet was doubled and then redoubled.

In this game, bids alternate, regardless of who wins

"A great golf hole is one which puts a question mark into the player's mind when he arrives on the tee to play it."
                    —Mackenzie Ross, golf course architect

the bid. Some golfers play this game with the bets automatically doubling in the event that: (1) the team that takes the bid not only achieves their bid but does so with both individual scores being lower than their two opponents' scores; or (2) the team that takes the bid achieves it but does so with a birdie or an eagle.

In Bridge, sometimes bidding to *not* take the bid is most important. Also, using bidding strategy to get your opponents to bid themselves into a tough position can be fun, and it allows you to escalate the betting by doubling. The thinking and the strategy on how you are going to bid is different on every hole.

BACKGAMMON or DOUBLE

This game is similar to Bridge, the big difference being the potential for betting runs through the entire hole. The game can be played individually or in teams, and it ends once every player has putted out. The low total score wins in this game; however, the betting can be distracting.

Using a team format as an example, this is how Backgammon is played: The team that starts off is said to have the "cube" and states that they will score a total of 9 on the par-4 hole. The other team accepts the bid and everyone then tees off. The team that made the bid apparently has hit one of their drives out of bounds or into the deep rough. As a result of the

> *"The number one thing in trouble is: don't get into more trouble!"*
> —Dave Stockton, *Golf* magazine, 1977

apparent difficulty in achieving a 9 for the hole, the other team doubles the first team, which means the bet is doubled. At this point, the first team can either accept the doubling and play on or admit that they can't achieve a 9 and concede the bet on this hole. Let's say that this team accepts the double and upon arriving at the ball in the rough, the teammates find it not only in bounds but also in a good lie with an open shot to the green. As a result, they double the bet again. The second team can either concede the bet on this hole or accept the bet, and then the match proceeds. After all the players have hit their shots, it appears that the first team has hit one ball over the green and the other into a trap, while the other team has left a ball short of the green and another on the green—but with a putt that is in three-putt range. The second team, seeing no trouble, then doubles the bet again. The first team again has the choice of conceding the match and not accepting the double and losing a total of 4 points each or of continuing. In this case they continue and accept the double, which is now 8 points. The first team put their third shots on the green with one ball five feet from the cup and the other two feet from the cup. The second team leaves both balls short of the hole by 10 and 15 feet. The first team, believing that they can sink at least one of their putts and that the other team won't, doubles the match. The second team thinks they can sink one of their putts and the teammates know that both the other players are poor putters, so they accept the double, which means they are now playing for 16 points. As it turns out, the first team misses both putts while the second team sinks one to end up with low total and win 16 points each on this hole—which is only the first hole of 18. If all the players had missed their putts, then they would have tied and there would have been no blood. If one player gets a shot on a hole, this can really influence the course of the betting as well as the strategy.

SIX, SIX, AND SIX or RANSOME

This is a two-player team game that is broken into three separate six-hole matches. On the first six holes, the best ball of the twosome counts; for the next six holes, the players play alternate shots until the ball is holed out with the low twosome score on each hole winning that hole; and for the final six holes, the aggregate score, or total score, of the twosome is used. In this game betting can be on an individual hole basis, which means that a total of 18 points can be won. Another way to bet this game is to have each six-hole format equal one bet so that a total of only three bets can be won or lost. This game can be played with full handicaps; if there is not a large discrepancy in handicaps, the teams can play even.

> *"If you keep shooting par at them, they all crack sooner or later."*
> —Bobby Jones

REJECT or WIPE-OUT

In this game, played either individually or on a four-ball basis, each player or team has the right to have the opponent replay four shots during the course of the round. Therefore, if you are playing four-ball teams the opponents have the right to have both you and your partner replay four shots, with your team having the same right. You might hit a great drive, cutting a dogleg and leaving only a short chip shot to the green, or possibly your partner hit a career shot to the green leaving the ball only inches from the cup for a sure birdie or eagle, or maybe you have sunk a long birdie putt—only to have your opponent or opposing team call for a replay. Sometimes *all* of the above occur, so this game can be either frustrating or funny, depending upon your perspective. The betting in this game can be either a straight medal game, a match game, or even a Nassau.

> *"Real golfers have two handicaps: one for braggin' and one for betting."*
> —Bob Irons, Red Bluff

THE SIDE GAMES WE PLAY & WAGER: GROUP FOUR

Other games we play are more of a golf outing, club function, or tournament nature. These types of games vary extensively in format but for the most part are fun to play. I have undoubtedly not included all the different types of golf formats available, but I believe that what is included will provide variety enough to plan games for a year or more.

You can have a prize for the team or group that wins each of these games, you can arrange to have your team play against another team, or you can be brave and bet the rest of the teams that your team will beat them. The wagering and betting are sometimes just as much fun as the playing.

So on to the games—again.

DROP OUT
THROW-OUT GAME or TOURNEY
SCOTCH TWOSOME
SCOTCH FOURSOME
FLAG TOURNAMENT or TOMBSTONE TOURNAMENT
CHICAGO SYSTEM
CALLAWAY SYSTEM
MODIFIED CALLAWAY SYSTEM
TIN WHISTLE PLAY or PAR/BOGEY PLAY
TWO-PLAYER SCRAMBLE
FOUR-PLAYER SCRAMBLE
HONEST JOHN RUSSELL
TWO-BALL FOURSOME

THE WHEEL
CRIER'S MATCH
LONG AND SHORT MATCH
ODD AND EVEN MATCH
BEST BALL CHAPMAN or BEST BALL PINEHURST
BEST BALL GREENSOME
BEST BALL GRUESOME
BEST BALL BLOODSOME
BEST BALL FENSOME
BEST BALL RYDER CUP
BONG
NO-ALIBI EVENT
SHAMBLE

DROP OUT

Utilizing full handicap and taking shots as they fall on the scorecard, in this game the players play against par. The winner is the player who can play the most holes in straight succession without losing to par. If a player shoots a bogey on the first hole and doesn't get a shot, then he or she is out of the match. This format is used until there is only one player left who has not lost a hole to par. Drop Out is most often played in conjunction with other types of games or bets. The winner wins the pot into which all players have put a predetermined amount of money. If you have a large field of players, you might even pay out to three or four places. It is surprising how many low handicappers bogey the first hole or first few holes because they are not sufficiently warmed up. Low handicappers do not always win in this game.

"The way I putted, I must've been reading the greens in Spanish and putting them in English."
—Homero Blancas, when asked to comment on his putting in the 1970 Masters

THROW-OUT GAME or TOURNEY

In this game a player may throw out the three worst holes so that only 15 holes are counted in determining score. This game is usually played with full handicap, thus resulting in a net 15-hole score. You usually bet this game based on the total 15-hole net score of each player. You may even arrange a Robin game so that you can play three five-hole matches.

"Tell me, do you chaps actually play this hole—or just photograph it?"
—Eustace Storey, British amateur, on his first look at the second hole of Pine Valley Golf Club, Cleminton, New Jersey

SCOTCH TWOSOME

In this game two players alternately hit the same ball until it is holed out. If, for example, Player A tees off on the first hole, a par 4, then Player B hits the second shot from wherever Player A's drive came to rest. If, however, Player A hits the ball out of bounds, then Player B retees hitting three. Continuing the example, and providing that Player A has not hit out of bounds, Player B hits the second shot and hits the green. Player A then putts and misses, leaving the ball short of the hole. Player B then putts and sinks the putt for a team score of a par 4. Going to the second tee, Player A tees off since Player B hit the last shot, or putted last. This is strictly a game in which the players hit or putt the ball on every other shot or putt regardless of what the player before has done.

SCOTCH FOURSOME

This game is played exactly the same as a Scotch Twosome but with four players. After selecting the order of play for each player, Player A tees off with Player B hitting next, and so on through C and D. If the ball has not been holed out after Player D, then Player A hits or putts again. The same order is maintained throughout the 18 holes of play. If Player C happens to hole out, then on the next tee Player D gets to tee off, followed by Player A, and so on. It's a game that keeps the entire team together throughout the 18 holes of play, and it can and does result in a lot of kidding and verbal harassment among team players. "Nice guy—you left me only a 30-foot putt!" Or,

"Thanks a lot, now I have to hit a shot over water." Or possibly, "That's great, what do I do with a fried-egg lie in the sand trap—I've never seen a lie like that, much less know how to hit it!"

FLAG TOURNAMENT or TOMBSTONE TOURNAMENT

In this contest each player is provided a small flag with his or her name attached. Using full handicaps, each player plays until he or she has used the number of strokes equaling par plus handicap, and at this point the player's flag is planted. If a player still has strokes left after 18 holes, then that player continues to play until all shots have been used, which in some cases might extend to two extra holes. The winner of this type of play is the player who plants the flag at the farthest point around the course.

In the case of playing a Tombstone Tournament, instead of flags each player should have a marker in the shape of a tombstone. Additionally, each tombstone, when planted, should have some type of humorous epitaph such as "Here John West expired" or "If it weren't for Dick Smith's duck hook, he would have survived longer" or "Mary Higgins died here because of three-putts!"

> *"It's good sportsmanship to not pick up lost golf balls while they are still rolling."*
> —Mark Twain

CHICAGO SYSTEM

This is a game that can also be played in conjunction with other matches or bets. In this game each player is given a predetermined point quota based on his or her handicap, as indicated here:

HCP	QUOTA	HCP	QUOTA	HCP	QUOTA	HCP	QUOTA
1	38	10	29	19	20	28	11
2	37	11	28	20	19	29	10
3	36	12	27	21	18	30	9
4	35	13	26	22	17	31	8
5	34	14	25	23	16	32	7
6	33	15	24	24	15	33	6
7	32	16	23	25	14	34	5
8	31	17	22	26	13	35	4
9	30	18	21	27	12	36	3

Points are scored for all players, regardless of handicap, as follows: bogey, 1 point; par, 2 points; birdie, 4 points; eagle, 8 points. The player whose point total for 18 holes most exceeds his or her point quota wins. If no one exceeds his or her point quota then the winner is the player who comes closest. Remember that in this game points are determined strictly on gross score, not on net score. The winner wins the pot, or, if you have a large number of players, you can pay out to third or fourth place.

Another way to play this game is that the low-point player of the foursome pays off the three players who have more points, and payoff is based upon whatever point value was predetermined times the differential in point totals. Besides the low-point player paying off, the player in third place also pays off the second-

place and first-place players, and the second-place-
point player pays off the player with the most points.
The payoffs are all based on the point differentials
among the players.

CALLAWAY SYSTEM

The Callaway System, a handicap system devised by
Lionel Callaway, the former head pro at Pinehurst,
North Carolina, applies to 18-hole regulation courses
only. This particular system allows for the handicap-
ping of players who do not have an established handicap, a system generally associated with large outings.
In this system a player's handicap is determined after
the completion of the round. The gross score of the
player determines the handicap adjustment by elimi-
nating a worst hole or worst holes and subtracting the
adjustment from the player's gross score.

The table that follows indicates the worst-hole de-
ductions that are allowed and an adjustment based
upon gross score. If for instance, a player shot a gross
score of 100, as the table indicates, that player can
deduct the three worst holes that were shot. In this
example, the player's three worst holes were a 9 and
two 8s, which adds up to a handicap of 25. This plus
the indicated adjustment of +2 results in a total handicap of 27. Therefore, this player's net score would be
100 minus 27, or 73. The following notes should also
be observed when using this system.

1. Maximum handicap allowed is 50.
2. No hole should be scored at more than two times
   its par.

3. Unless you are using a shotgun format, the 17th and 18th holes should never be deducted.
4. Half strokes count as a whole stroke.
5. In case of ties and no scorecard playoff, the lower handicap or adjustment is given preference.

Score					Deductions for Handicap
		70	71	72	Scratch and adjustment
73	74	75			½ worst hole and adjustment
76	77	78	79	80	1 worst hole and adjustment
81	82	83	84	85	1½ worst holes and adjustment
86	87	88	89	90	2 worst holes and adjustment
91	92	93	94	95	2½ worst holes and adjustment
96	97	98	99	100	3 worst holes and adjustment
101	102	103	104	105	3½ worst holes and adjustment
106	107	108	109	110	4 worst holes and adjustment
111	112	113	114	115	4½ worst holes and adjustment
116	117	118	119	120	5 worst holes and adjustment
121	122	123	124	125	5½ worst holes and adjustment
126	127	128	129	130	6 worst holes and adjustment

Adjustment

−2 −1 0 +1 +2 deduct or add to
                   handicap

MODIFIED CALLAWAY SYSTEM

Since par-3 golf courses have different scoring requirements than regulation 18-hole courses, the Callaway System has been adapted to account for this difference using the following format for play on 18-hole par-3 courses.

1. Half strokes count as the next highest whole number.
2. Unless using a shotgun start, do not deduct scores for the 17th and 18th holes.
3. In the case of ties where a scorecard playoff is not used, the low handicap takes preference.

Score	Deduct
54 and below	Scratch, no adjustment
55–57	½ worst hole
58–62	1 worst hole
63–67	1½ worst holes
68–72	2 worst holes
73–77	2½ worst holes
78–82	3 worst holes
83–87	3½ worst holes
88–92	4 worst holes
93–97	4½ worst holes
98–102	5 worst holes
103–107	5½ worst holes
108–110	6 worst holes

TIN WHISTLE PLAY or PAR/BOGEY PLAY

This is another game involving points that are re-
warded based upon a player's score and is somewhat
similar in nature to a Stableford or a Hogan game. In
this game, however, points are awarded based upon
the following: 1 point for each hole that is made in
one over par, 3 points for each hole that is parred, and
5 points for each hole on which a birdie is scored.
This game is played with full handicap so that a hole
on which a player has a stroke would count as a birdie
if the player scored a par on the hole and would
therefore earn 5 points. The player who has the most
points at the end of the round wins the pot or the
point differential between the other players times the
value, as decided earlier, of each point. This game is
reputed to have originated with some Pinehurst
golfers known as the Tin Whistles.

TWO-PLAYER SCRAMBLE

This involves two players as a team, both playing their
own shots and then continually selecting the best ball
of the two, including putts, until the ball is holed out.
As an example, Player A and Player B both tee off on
the first hole, which is a par 4. Player A hooks the ball
into the rough while Player B hits a drive into the
middle of the fairway a good distance off the tee.
Selecting Player B's drive, both Player A and Player B
hit their second shots to the green from the spot of
Player B's drive, and they again select the best shot
from which to proceed. In our example, Player B
pushes the shot into the greenside sand trap while

Player A has hit a shot 15 feet from the pin. Selecting Player A's ball, both players putt from where Player A's ball is. Player A putts first and putts the ball three feet past the pin. Player B putts and leaves the putt just a few inches short of the hole. Selecting Player B's putt, Player B then putts out sinking the putt for a team score of par 4. If Player B had sunk the putt, and not left it short, after Player A had putted, then the team score would have been a birdie 3. In this game, if a player inadvertently taps in a putt before the partner has had a chance to putt, then the hole is considered to be completed, and the partner does not get to putt.

FOUR-PLAYER SCRAMBLE

This game is just like a Two-Player Scramble, except that it involves four players. Each player tees off and the best drive is selected and then all players hit their second shots from within 12 inches of the best drive. This format is used on each series of shots or putts, always selecting the best shot or putt of the four, until the ball is holed out. Remember that if the first, second, or third putter has not holed out and by force of habit taps in the putt after missing the original putt, the remaining players do not putt, as the hole is considered to be completed. So if a putt is missed, regardless of how close it is, mark it until all have putted.

As an equalizer in this type of game, it is common to mix both high and low handicappers together on the same team. I have played in games that require that each player's drive be used on at least three or four holes of the 18. With this in mind, it is sometimes better to use a high handicapper's drive that is only 175 yards off the tee but in the fairway, rather than a low handicapper's drive that is 275 yards off the tee. Strategy in selecting shots, especially drives, can be crucial to how the team scores.

HONEST JOHN RUSSELL

This is a game in which each player predicts what his or her final score will be prior to teeing off. The maximum score allowed on holes 17 and 18 are bogeys. The player or players whose score is closest to that predicted wins the total pot. The pot is determined by each player contributing 1 unit of the bet for each stroke under the predicted score or 1 unit for each stroke over.

> *"Caddies are a breed of their own. If you shoot a 66, they say, 'Man, we shot a 66!' But go out and shoot a 77 and they say, 'Hell, he shot a 77!'"*
> —Lee Trevino, *They Call Me Super Mex,* 1982

TWO-BALL FOURSOME

In this game two players are a team and use only one ball, and partners alternate in playing the shots. One partner drives from all the odd-numbered tees and the other partner drives from all the even-numbered tees regardless of which partner hit the last shot or made the last putt.

If there is not a large discrepancy in handicaps among the four players, this game can be played as a straight gross score. If, however, there is a major difference in handicaps, then usually one-half of the combined handicaps is used to provide some parity. This game can be played by two twosomes or by an entire field of players that could consist of 72 twosomes. If you are playing another twosome you can arrange almost any type of bet, whether a medal game, match game, or even a Nassau game. If there are more than two twosomes you can arrange a bet with the other twosomes, or everyone can agree that each team puts into the common pot a set amount of money, with the winning twosome taking the pot. If there are more than eight twosomes then you can split the pot and pay out as many places as you decide upon.

> *"Golf is not a game you can rush. For every stroke you try to force out of her, she is going to extract two strokes in return."*
> —Dave Hill, *Teed Off,* 1977

THE WHEEL

This game is played, using full handicaps, in a best ball twosome format. With a minimum of 16 players, each player can select from one up to a maximum of three other players as partners and pay a set amount of money for each partner selected into a common pot or kitty. At the end of 18 holes, the players then compare their scorecards with their partners' to determine the lowest net score for each hole. The player who has the lowest score wins the pot and any other money that might have been bet by the other players. Once again, with a large field it is common to pay out as many places as are agreed upon before play.

CRIER'S MATCH

This game can be either a straight match, in which you play hole by hole with or without handicap, or a medal match, in which you compare your total score, gross or net, to your competitor's. Each player gets to pick out his or her two or possibly three worst holes compared to par, and revert these scores back to par. If you are playing teams, then the same format is still used, with the team's worst two or three holes reverting back to par before it's decided who has won the match. This type of play can have some interesting results. If you play with someone who is always saying, "If I hadn't shot this or that on those two holes I would have beaten you," well, this is a game in which you can give that person a chance to prove it!

LONG AND SHORT MATCH

The game is called this name for lack of a better one. Since some players have better long games than short games, and vice versa, this game combines the ability of both types of players. For instance, you might be straight and long off the tee and hit your irons the same way, but once you get around the green or have to hit a pitch shot, you have the touch of a gorilla! However, you know another player who, if his or her life depended upon it, couldn't drive or hit irons but has an amazing touch around the greens. In this case, you would drive and hit all the long irons while your partner would hit all the approach shots and do all the putting. The type of bet you make in this game often depends upon the faith you have in your partner.

ODD AND EVEN MATCH

This is played twosome against twosome, or with as many twosomes as want to bet. In this game one player of the team plays all the even holes, and the partner plays all the odd holes. Usually only one-half of the combined handicap is utilized to determine the net score of each twosome, with low net score winning. This game can be played at the same time you are playing other games, such as a Nassau. Just decide whose score will be used on the odd and even holes and then play your regular game with everyone playing all 18 holes.

BEST BALL CHAPMAN or BEST BALL PINEHURST

In this best ball game (involving teams of two players), both partners drive and then both hit their second shots and then decide which ball to play for the third shot regardless of whether it is an iron shot or a putt. The player whose second shot was not selected is the player to hit the third shot, with the partners then alternating every shot until the ball is holed out. This format is followed for the entire round of golf. This game is usually played with one-half of the team's total handicap and, depending upon the type of game you are playing, the handicap can be deducted from the gross score or the handicap strokes can be taken where they fall on the scorecard.

BEST BALL GREENSOME

In this format, two partners both drive and then select the best drive from which to hit the second shot. The drive that is not selected is that of the partner who hits the second shot, and the partners alternate hitting the shots until the ball is holed out. This same format is used on all subsequent holes. One-half of the team's total handicap is used to derive a net score or, if involved in a match format, the handicap strokes are applied where they fall on the scorecard.

> *"The best swing we have is our practice swing. Unfortunately we never use it."*
> —Ken Venturi, *PGA* magazine, 1990

BEST BALL GRUESOME

In this game one twosome plays against another two-some; the opposing twosome selects which drive of the other twosome is to be played, naturally choosing the worst drive. Once the drives have been selected each player of the twosome plays out the hole. This game can be played as either the best ball of the twosome or the total score of the twosome.

BEST BALL BLOODSOME

In this twosome game both partners hit their tee shots, and the opposing twosome selects which shot of the two will be played for the second shot. As in Best Ball Gruesome, the opposing twosome naturally selects the worst drive, and the player whose drive was not selected hits the second shot. Play then proceeds, with each partner hitting or putting alternately until the ball is holed out. In this game the best ball wins the hole.

BEST BALL FENSOME

In this twosome game both partners drive and then select the best drive from which to hit their second shot. However, in the Fensome format one player hits all the second shots on the odd-numbered holes while the other player hits all the second shots on the even-numbered holes, regardless of whose drive was se-lected. After the second shot has been played, the partners then alternate shots or putts until the ball is holed out. One-half the team's total handicap is used to determine a net score or, if in a match format, the handicap strokes are applied where they fall on the scorecard.

BEST BALL RYDER CUP

In this format each team consists of two players, with each player driving on either all the odd-numbered holes or the even-numbered holes. The player who does not drive is the player who hits the second shot, and the players alternate hitting the shots or putting the ball until it is holed out.

This is the format that the pros play, and therefore it is a format best suited for good players, mainly because of the demands placed upon the player driving the ball.

BONG

This is a game in which mishaps or errant shots are assigned points known as Bong points. The player at the end of 18 holes having the highest number of Bong points pays the other players the difference in their point totals. The Bong points are as follows: lost ball, 2 points; out of bounds, 2 points; in the sand trap, 1 point; in the water or water hazard, 1 point; two shots to get out of a sand trap, 3 points; hitting from one sand trap into another, 2 points; and three-putting, 2 points. So in this game it's very important to try to keep your shots straight!

NO-ALIBI EVENT

In this game, instead of deducting a player's handicap at the end of the round, each player is allowed to replay or rehit (during the round) the number of shots equal to three-fourths of his or her handicap. Some people play using full handicaps. A stroke that is replayed must be used even if it is worse than the original shot, and it cannot be replayed a second time. The replay can also apply to putts. This game can be played individually, with the low score winning, or with teams, playing either a best ball or total score for the twosome or foursome.

SHAMBLE

This is a point game in which a foursome plays as a team to accumulate as many points as possible against the rest of the field. In Shamble everyone on the team hits a tee shot and then the foursome selects the best drive. From the spot of the best drive, each player in the foursome hits the second shot and continues to play out the hole. Players in this game use their full handicaps, with points earned individually based upon the following: 1 point for par, 2 points for a birdie, 3 points for an eagle, and 4 points for a double eagle. Points are totaled on each hole for all four players, and the team with the highest point total at the end of the round is the winner. The points won are based on net scores of each individual player, which allows each player to contribute to the game.

This is also a game that tends to favor the higher-handicap player, and with this format players often find that they are able to shoot scores that are five to ten shots better than normal. It is also a game format that brings everyone together as a team, with each player pulling for the other.

THE 19TH HOLE

Well, I hope the games that have been described here won't get you into trouble. They are not intended to; rather, the intention is to provide you the opportunity for more fun, competition, and social intercourse while on the course. Remember, we do not play the game for a living and therefore firmly believe that a good part of the game is the company you play with.

Regardless of who buys the drinks or who wins or loses, good company provides the theater to commiserate about that poor shot or poor round or, on the other hand, to relive a great shot or a great round by explaining it again and again. Enjoy the game and the company you play with.

Finally, I realize that in all likelihood there are other games that people play or variations to the games that have been described that I have not included in this book. That is because I have not played them or have not heard about them. If you play a game, or have a variation of a game that has not been described, please drop me a line and let me know about that game.

Write to us at:

Dogleg Publications
4601 E. Skyline Dr. #801
P.O. Box 64209
Tucson, AZ 85728-1209

When writing please advise us of the name of the game and how it is played. Include your name and address and a telephone number where we can reach you. Thanks.

> *"Golf is a game of inches. The most important are those between the ears."*
> —Arnold Palmer

THE GAMBLING POLICY OF THE UNITED STATES GOLF ASSOCIATION AND THE ROYAL AND ANCIENT GOLF CLUB OF ST. ANDREWS, SCOTLAND

The Definition of an Amateur Golfer provides that an amateur golfer is one who plays the game as a non-remunerative or non-profit-making sport. When gambling motives are introduced, problems can arise which threaten the integrity of the game.

The USGA does not object to participation in wagering among individual golfers or teams of golfers when participation in the wagering is limited to the players, the players may only wager on themselves or their teams, the sole source of all money won by players is advanced by the players and the primary purpose is the playing of the game for enjoyment.

The distinction between playing for prize money and gambling is essential to the validity of the Rules of Amateur Status. The following constitute golf wagering and not playing for prize money. 1. Participation in wagering among individual golfers. 2. Participation in wagering among teams.

Organized amateur events open to the general golfing public and designed and promoted to create cash prizes are not approved by the USGA. Golfers participating in such events without irrevocably waiving their right to cash prizes are deemed by the USGA to be playing for prize money.

The USGA is opposed to and urges its Member Clubs, all golf associations and all other sponsors of golf competitions to prohibit types of gambling such as: (1) Calcuttas, (2) other auction pools, (3) paramutuals and (4) other forms of gambling organized for general participation or permitting participants to bet on someone other than themselves or their teams.

The Association may deny amateur status, entry in USGA Championships and membership on USGA teams for international competitions to players whose activities in connection with golf gambling, whether organized or individual, are considered by the USGA to be contrary to the best interests of golf.

INDEX OF GAMES

Animals   13

Arnies   8

Australian Hogan   60

Automatics   95

Average Score   92

Backgammon   120

Barkies   8

Best Ball Bloodsome   149

Best Ball Chapman   148

Best Ball Fensome   149

Best Ball Foursome   91

Best Ball Greensome   148

Best Ball Gruesome   149

Best Ball Pinehurst   148

Best Ball Ryder Cup   150

Bingo-Bango-Bongo   4

Bingle-Bangle-Bungle   4

Blind-Draw Best Ball   65

Blue-Plate Special   5

BMWs   6

Bogey   66
Bong   150
Bridge   117
British Stableford   51
Callaway System   137
Captain   109
Carpets   6
Center or Right   86
Chairman   56
Chicago System   136
Chicken and Snake   6
Coyote Kill   56
Crier's Match   146
Daytona   108
DBs   67
Dog, The   116
Double   120
Double Bogey   67
Double Murphys   12
Drop Out   130
East Coast Point Game   55
Eclectic   95
18-Hole Greenies   7
Eighty-One   96
Every Three Holes   94
Exotic Sandies   8
Ferrets   10
Fivesome Games
    Every Three Holes   94
    Fivesome Wheel   90
    Wolf and Pig Fivesome   114

Fivesome Wheel   90
Flag Tournament   134
Flaggy   15
Four-Ball Foursome   87
Four-Player Scramble   142
Garbarge   4
Garbarge Skins   10
Golden Ferrets   10
Greenies   5
Gritties   7
Hawk   109
Hog   113
Hogans   8
Hogan Point Game   60
Honest John Russell   143
Joker Stableford   54
Las Vegas   105
Las Vegas, AZ   108
Long and Short Match   147
Low Balls of Foursome   90
Low Net Foursome   63
Low Putts   19
Match Play   34
Match Play Handicap   35
Medal Play   30
Medal Play Handicap   30
Moles   10
Modified Callaway System   139
Murphys   12
Nassau   38
Nassau Four Ways   46

Nassau—Partners   42
Nassau—Partners—Low Ball,
    High Ball   43
Nassau—Partners—Low Ball,
    Low Total   43
Nassau Six Ways   46
Nicklauses   12
Nines   96
No-Alibi Event   151
Odd and Even Match   147
One-Half Aggregate Score   86
Ouzle-Fouzle   7
Par/Bogey Play   140
Parrot   56
Per Yard Per Hole   63
Plonkers   5
Point a Hole   63
Point Game   61
Poley   15
Press   40
Proxies   5
Rabbit   24
Rabbits   25
Ransome   123
Reject   124
Robbins   47
Robbins Nassau   47
Roll the Drums   40
Sandies   7
Scotch Foursome   133
Scotch Twosome   133

Scruffies   13

Seven-Eleven   19

Seven-Point Game   62

Seven-Up   18

Sevies   8

Shamble   151

Six-Hole Switch   47

Six, Six, and Six   123

Sixes   47

Sixteens   104

Skins   16

Snake   22

Snakes   22

Stableford   51

Stroke Play   30

Super Sandies   7

Tee Game   24

Threesome Games

   Chairman   56

   Eighty-One or Nines   96

   One-Half Aggregate Score   86

   Parrot   56

   The Dog   116

   Threesome Hawk   112

   Threesome Six-Point Game   54

Threesome Hawk   112

Throw-Out Game   131

Ticks   25

Tin Whistle Play   140

Titanic   13

Tombstone Tournament   134

Tourney   131
Twelves   100
Twenty-One   26
Two-Ball Foursome   144
Two-Player Scramble   140
Umbrella   26
Walk Walk   22
Watsons   10
Wheel, The   146
Wipe-Out   124
Wolf   109
Wolf and Pig Fivesome   114
Woodies   8
Yardages   63